D0016228

WITHDRAWN

WITHDRAWN

PHILOSOPHY IN BITE-SIZED CHUNKS

PHILOSOPHY

IN BITE-SIZED CHUNKS

Bridger Public Library

LESLEY LEVENE

METRO BOOKS
New York

METRO BOOKS
New York

An Imprint of Sterling Publishing Co., Inc.
1166 Avenue of the Americas
New York, NY 10036

METRO BOOKS and the distinctive Metro Books logo are
registered trademarks of Sterling Publishing Co., Inc.

Text and illustrations © 2017 by Michael O'Mara Books

All rights reserved. No part of this publication may be reproduced,
stored in a retrieval system, or transmitted in any form or by any
means (including electronic, mechanical, photocopying, recording, or
otherwise) without prior written permission from the publisher.

ISBN 978-1-4351-6770-4

For information about custom editions, special sales, and premium
and corporate purchases, please contact Sterling Special Sales at
800-805-5489 or specialsales@sterlingpublishing.com.

Manufactured in the UK

2 4 6 8 10 9 7 5 3 1

www.sterlingpublishing.com

Credits: Cover design by Claire Cater; Illustrations by
Andrew Pinder; designed and typeset by Glen Saville

For Jose and Cyril Levene
and Ruth and Peter Spencer –
all of whom have good reason to view
life philosophically

Contents

What's It All About, Then?

'All are lunatics, but he who can analyze his delusion is called a philosopher.'
— Ambrose Bierce, *Epigrams*

The very fact that this book ranges over some two and a half thousand years suggests the answer: that there is no answer. What is clear, however, is that people have been asking philosophical questions in an effort to understand the world and their role in it for as long as records have existed.

In the introduction to his *History of Western Philosophy*, Bertrand Russell points out that philosophy straddles the fields of science and theology, attempting to apply human reason to speculations in areas where definite knowledge is not yet available. The fascinating thing is that, as more knowledge becomes available, the questions still remain. Which is fine, because there's nothing like a bit of healthy speculation – as long as you are well informed.

By looking at the development of philosophical ideas over time, placing individual philosophers against their historical and social backgrounds to get a sense of what was influencing their thinking, this book aims to provide you with the wherewithal to speculate with the best of them.

I would like to thank Louise Dixon and Silvia Crompton at Michael O'Mara Books for their patience throughout, and various friends – especially Annie Lee, Richard Sandover and Peter Spencer – who have helped by providing advice, books and a sympathetic ear or two. Moreover, I hereby swear that, in my other life as an editor, I will never again moan about authors who deliver their books late.

THE PRESOCRATIC PHILOSOPHERS

◎◎

The name says it all: the Presocratics were around before Socrates. A number of early thinkers from the ancient world, some of whom might even have known of his ideas, can be grouped together under this heading. Dating from the late seventh century to the fifth century BC, they all attempted in their different ways to explain how the world was constituted and to explore the nature of reality. In other words, they were trying to answer the great 'What's it all about, then?' question.

The earliest Presocratic philosophers came from Ionia, midway along the west coast of Asia Minor. The area, which is now part of Turkey, had been colonized by the Greeks from about 1000 BC and, by the time our Presocratics came along, was home to a number of flourishing city-states. These prospered as a result of trade and cultural links with Egypt and Babylonia (present-day Iraq) to the east, both renowned for their ancient wisdom, as well as with the Greek colonies on the Black Sea and the Greek mainland further west. Moreover, Ionia had a literary heritage linking it via Homer to the riches of Mycenae.

Such conditions must have fostered a vigorous intellectual life, because there certainly seems to have been much interest in speculative thought in the major centres of population – Miletus, Ephesus, Colophon and Samos – and great thinkers from here, together with their ideas, gradually began to exert an influence that spread into the world beyond.

⚭

Thales

(c. 624–c. 545 BC)

According to Aristotle, who presumably knew what he was talking about, Thales of Miletus was the first real philosopher, which makes him the founder not just of Greek but ultimately of European philosophy. Unhelpfully, he left behind no body of work, so his opinions are known only from later reports, but he seems to have had wide-ranging practical and intellectual interests, and was renowned as an engineer, a mathematician, an astronomer and a statesman. He is said to have travelled to Egypt, where he pursued his interest in trigonometry – it was presumably some sort of mathematical hot spot – and to have used Babylonian celestial charts to accurately predict a solar eclipse in 585 BC.

What makes it possible to talk about Thales and the later Presocratics as philosophers – rather than, say, brilliant mathematicians or astronomers – is the fact that they believed the world had an underlying unity, something physical that could be pinned down, studied and understood rationally, in order to identify how it had come into being. Of course, there was one small snag: they had no idea what this miraculous substance was.

There would be plenty of false starts, but the search itself signalled a move away from mythology as an explanation for events. Rather than looking to the frankly irrational behaviour of the gods to answer questions about why things were as they were, these early philosophers attempted to come up with systematic accounts of the visible world in straightforward descriptive and analytical terms.

For Thales, water was the key. Having seen the way it could take on different forms (mist, ice and so on), he decided that water must be the basis of the universe – literally, in fact, since he thought that the flat earth floated on water and that earthquakes were caused when big waves hit the land.

He was cited as one of the 'Seven Wise Men' by Plato in his *Protagoras*, but was more the absent-minded professor in a number of anecdotes, such as the one that had him stumbling into a ditch because he was too busy studying the stars to watch where he was going.

෨෧

Anaximander

(610–546 BC)

Born in Miletus, Anaximander was quite possibly a pupil of Thales. Like Thales, he had a number of scientific interests: he produced the first (admittedly wildly inaccurate) map of the world, he studied meteorology (declaring that thunder was the banging together of clouds) and he introduced the gnomon (the upright arm of the sundial) to the Greek world. A statesman, too, he was chosen as leader of his city's new Black Sea colony, Apollonia. He was also Thales' successor on the philosophical front, actually writing down his ideas – another first – although he disagreed with the premise that water, or indeed any one physical element, could be the first principle.

Anaximander argued that if water were given pre-eminence, other elements such as fire would be excluded: while water might change into mist and ice, it could not encompass the opposites wet and dry. He preferred to look for a more universal originating substance, one that was not bounded by physical characteristics. He came up with the notion of 'the indefinite', *apeiron*, from which all things are created and to which all things return, and suggested that the universe and all its elements and opposites came into being only when separation from the indefinite took place.

To be more specific, Anaximander said that, when heat and cold had escaped from the *apeiron*, the heavier cold mist had solidified to form the earth – which is a broad cylinder that sits unsupported at the centre of the universe – while the heat had expanded out into huge wheels of flame circling the earth. The air between the earth and the fire creates a mist, and it is only through gaps in this mist that we can perceive chinks of light from the fiery wheels – or what we now know to be stars and planets. Within the world, pairs of linked opposites – wet/dry, hot/cold, etc. – resulting from the initial separation

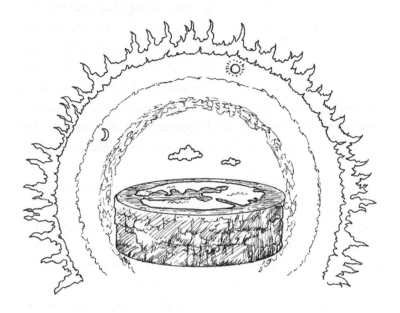

constantly seek to return to the indefinite, providing rhythm and unity to the universe.

Among Anaximander's other interesting ideas were that the orderly process that produced the world visible to him was equally likely to be producing other worlds he knew nothing of, and that human beings – who originally had spines on their skin, like fish – had emerged from the slime left behind once the waters drew back from the land. In short, the early Presocratic obsession with water was still very much alive.

೧೦

Anaximenes

(fl. c. 545 BC, d. 528 BC)

There's a third one from Miletus, though sadly no biographical details about him exist. Anaximenes seems to have reverted to Thales' idea that there was one basic form of matter – in this case, *aer* (air or mist) – but he proposed that this single substance could be transformed into other substances according to its degree of concentration. Rarefied it became fire; condensed it formed water and earth. As well as making the obvious links with the physical world (the sun as fire in the sky, lightning emerging from clouds, mist falling as rain), Anaximenes connected air with the breath of life, the soul, thus drawing upon Anaximander's 'indefinite'. For Anaximenes, the earth was flat and floated on the air like a leaf, as did the heavenly bodies, fiery discs that had been formed from rarefied rising vapour.

೧೦

Pythagoras

(c. 570–*c.* 490 BC)

Born on the Greek island of Samos, Pythagoras – yes, he of the theorem: the square of the hypotenuse etc., etc. – is said to have visited both Egypt and Babylonia before settling at

Croton, a Greek colony in southern Italy, in about 530 BC. Here he established a community that eventually became both a mathematical school and a religious group. As he left behind no written works, most of what we know about Pythagoras comes from later accounts, many of which were obviously embellished over time, assuming the form of myths and legends. Among other things, he is described as having a golden thigh and is credited with the ability to be in two places at once, as well as to project writing from a mirror on to the moon.

On a more practical level, Pythagoras observed that musical notes differed according to the different lengths of an instrument's strings, deducing from this that mathematical ratios were what underpinned musical harmony (in the process also introducing the concept of musical intervals). From there he went on to assert that mathematics lay at the heart of reality – not water, not air, but numbers. It was numbers that defined (think of Anaximander's 'indefinite') the shapes and forms of physical objects, just as they determined the movement of the stars and other celestial bodies, a harmonious mathematical relationship known as the music of the spheres.

From here, Pythagoreanism developed as much as a way of life as a philosophy. Its adherents favoured a contemplative, abstemious lifestyle, living communally, with men and women treated equally and property held in common. They were seeking their own form of earthly harmony through moral asceticism and ritual purification of the body (beans were strictly off limits, as was meat) and the soul. Pythagoras held that all living things were related and believed in the transmigration of souls – in other words, that the soul was immortal and passed on to a different body after death – claiming that he had been other people in earlier lives.

Many of Pythagoras' ideas later found expression in the writings of Plato, most obviously the emphasis on a pure reality – as manifested for Pythagoras in mathematics and the immortality of the soul – underlying imperfect appearances.

☙❧

Xenophanes
(c. 570–c. 475 BC)

It was probably in 546 BC, when the victorious armies of Cyrus the Great swept through Asia Minor, absorbing the Greek city-states of Ionia into the Persian Empire, that Xenophanes left his home in Colophon. For the rest of his life he wandered around the Mediterranean, basing himself for a time in Sicily and also visiting Elea in southern Italy, home to an important group of philosophers with whom he was later linked. He wrote poetry, fragments of which survive, and these, together with references in other people's works, give us an idea of his wide-ranging interests.

Xenophanes posed one of the most knotty and enduring of philosophical questions: how can any of us honestly claim to know the truth about things we haven't seen for ourselves? In other words, he pointed out that there's a big difference between opinion and true knowledge, and that, while truth exists, we can only speculate about it. From there, he turned his attention to a whole host of topics.

On the religious front, rather than rejecting random acts by the gods as an explanation for events, he actively criticized the traditional Homeric approach of attributing our human failings – adultery, theft, deceit (so no change there) – to the gods. Xenophanes argued not only that this endorsed immoral behaviour, but also that such anthropomorphism – the giving of human characteristics to non-humans – led to logical absurdities. It was confusing enough that Ethiopians had black-haired gods and Thracians red-haired ones, but what about horses and cattle – how would their gods look? Instead, he suggested that there was a single supreme deity, spherical like the world, eternal and unchanging, totally different from humans in appearance and nature, who operated through the power of his mind.

Pursuing his interest in promoting moral behaviour among his fellow citizens, Xenophanes also spoke out against excessive drinking, the acquisition of unnecessary luxuries and the ludicrous honours heaped on successful athletes – all of which sounds remarkably familiar. Less so, and on a more down-to-earth level, when he saw fossils of fish far from the sea, he concluded that the earth had once been covered by water, going on to propose that earth and water in various combinations formed the basis of all things, with clouds a transitional state.

◎◎

Heraclitus

(*c.* 535–475 BC)

Born in Ephesus into an established aristocratic family, Heraclitus seems to have had no interest in participating in public life, refusing favours from the Persian authorities on the grounds that he did not care for luxury. He obviously had even less interest in making himself popular – he was forever accusing people of stupidity, going so far as to single out Xenophanes as someone who had no sense despite all his learning. He is believed to have written a book called *On Nature*, of which only fragments remain, and these, together with the responses of other writers to his work, give us some idea of his opinions.

Heraclitus is best known for his rather baffling assertion that everything exists in a state of permanent flux, so it is little wonder that he gained the nickname 'The Obscure'. As he explained it, you can never step into the same river twice for the simple reason that the water you dip your toes into on the second occasion is not the same water you touched the first time round. The world might *appear* to be a stable, unified whole – which was what prompted Thales, Anaximander and others to look for a single unifying component – but Heraclitus felt that this was to miss the point. Rather than seeing permanence and stability, he declared that, beneath the surface, the world could be understood in terms of a continuous struggle between pairs of opposites. The examples he gave ranged from the fairly pedestrian – up/down, hot/cold, wet/dry, day/night – to the down-right extreme: life/death, war/peace, famine/plenty. Although each part of the pair was separate, neither could exist without the other, as both were merely extreme aspects of the same thing. These opposites shared a common structural feature, which Heraclitus called *logos* (reason), and it was this that, like a form of eternal cosmic justice, maintained some sort of balance and regulated the continuity of change.

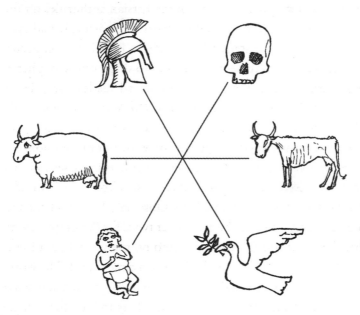

For Heraclitus, then, the unity of the world existed in its underlying structure – the way it was arranged – rather than in any particular component. He did, however, identify fire as the original and most desirable element, and the physical manifestation of *logos*.

❧

Parmenides

(*c.* 515–450 BC)

Born in the Greek colony of Elea, southern Italy, Parmenides is generally seen as the brains behind the Eleatic school, which emphasized the unchanging nature of reality. His early life is not well documented, but at the age of sixty-five he apparently met the young Socrates, whose ideas – and by extension those of Plato – he certainly seems to have influenced. Parmenides was the first philosopher to use logic and language to reach conclusions about the world that didn't rely on observation, and indeed often flew directly in the face of it.

His opinions have come down to us through the surviving 150 or so lines of a much longer three-part poem called – once again – *On Nature*. In the first part, he describes meeting a goddess who promises to reveal to him both 'the way of truth', or reality, and 'the way of seeming', or opinion; these then form the second and third parts of the poem. Basically, as far as reality goes, if we can think and talk about something, logic says it must exist – it *is* – since it makes no sense to think or talk about something that doesn't exist, and which *is not*.

If you can get your head around that, explains Parmenides, it surely follows that there was nothing before (the past) and there is nothing to come (the future), as both imply non-being in the present, and this in turn means that there has never been and never will be any change. So, things continue in some sort of eternal, static, uniform present. There can be no motion, because that would imply a move into nothingness; there can be no material change, because that would imply the existence of a previous state. All of which leads to the conclusion that any sort of change we *think* we see must be illusory: the way of seeming rather than the way of truth.

The reasoning might seem artificial – whatever Parmenides' grip on logic, his argument relies on a mind-boggling interpretation of the verb 'to be' – but the conflict between reality and illusion is real enough, and it's one that has continued to exercise philosophers ever since.

◎◎

Anaxagoras

(*c.* 500–428 BC)

Originally from Clazomenae in Ionia, Anaxagoras spent thirty years in Athens, the first philosopher to bring this brand of intellectual enquiry to what was to become the centre of the ancient Greek world. Here his teachings influenced, among others, the statesman Pericles and the playwright Euripides. When asked the point of being born, his answer was 'to study the universe'. Eventually these studies led him to assert that the sun was a huge incandescent lump of rock bigger than the Peloponnese, a pronouncement that seems to have upset the authorities, as he was prosecuted for impiety, convicted and subsequently banished.

REDUCTIO AD ABSURDUM: ZENO'S PARADOXES

A follower of Parmenides – he of the static, unchanging universe – Zeno of Elea (*c.* 490–430 BC) came up with a number of teasing paradoxes to demonstrate the impossibility of motion.

Take Achilles and the tortoise for starters: speedy Greek superhero vs. ambling slowcoach. Well, Achilles might be faster, but if he begins the race 100 metres behind the tortoise, the tortoise will have shuffled on a bit further by the time Achilles has made up the ground. And even though the tortoise is now ahead by only a short distance, Achilles still needs to catch up with him before he can overtake. Every time Achilles reaches the tortoise's previous position, the tortoise will once again have made some small progress. Breaking the task down into infinitesimal pieces – something Zeno just loved to do – Achilles will forever have just a little bit further to run in order to catch up with the tortoise. This is all nonsense, of course, but philosophically speaking, Zeno has a point.

Using the same logic, Zeno explained why it's impossible to cross from one side of a racecourse to the other. Before you can cover the whole distance, you need to cover half, and half again, and again – in other words, there are so many increasingly tiny journeys to make that you'll get nowhere fast.

Then there's the one with the arrow. You line up your target, you take aim, you fire … But at any point during its flight, your arrow is occupying the whole of a tiny bit of space, and is, in that instant, motionless. Given that its so-called 'flight' is made up of a succession of motionless instances, presumably, says Zeno, the arrow is not actually moving at all.

Zeno met Socrates on a trip to Athens with Parmenides, as a result of which he featured in Plato's dialogue *Parmenides*, and was credited by Aristotle as being the first to use dialectic – a formal method of disputation in which opponents attempted to find inconsistencies and absurdities in each other's arguments. Which brings us back to those paradoxes again.

To arrive at his own interpretation of the material world, Anaxagoras took Parmenides' assertion that things did not come into being or pass away and attempted to reconcile it with the visible evidence of change that existed everywhere around. The result was his theory that the world had originally consisted of all kinds of natural particles mixed together, before *nous* (mind) – 'the finest of all things and the purest', the driving force – started it spinning. In the vortex that ensued, the various particles combined and separated to create all manner of things, meaning that there would always be a small portion of everything in everything else – apart, that is, from in *nous*, which is 'mixed with nothing'. While each object's main constituent at any given time would define its identity, the ongoing combination and separation of spinning particles made change not only possible, but also inevitable.

With his introduction of *nous* as the prime mover, Anaxagoras was providing a purely mechanistic explanation of how things operated. Later philosophers would take his ideas a stage further and begin to look for an underlying sense of purpose as well.

◎◎

Empedocles
(c. 495–c. 435 BC)

Born in the Greek colony Acragas (modern Agrigento) in Sicily, Empedocles gained fame not only as a philosopher and poet, but also as a doctor, a scientist and a statesman. Legend credits him with higher aspirations, too, for he is said to have thrown himself into the crater on Mount Etna to prove his godlike nature – unfortunately, according to the verse quoted by Bertrand Russell in his *History of Western Philosophy*, Empedocles' last experiment ended then and there, as he was 'roasted whole'.

His main philosophical work is the poem called – yes, you guessed – *On Nature*, many fragments of which survive. Where Parmenides saw a static, permanently unchanging universe and Anaxagoras a universe created from an unlimited number of substances mixed together, Empedocles held that all things were made from four basic and permanent elements or 'roots': earth, air, fire and water. Influenced by twin forces that he called Love and Strife, these elements would come together and pull apart to form different objects. The universe moved through a never-ending cycle: first Love dominated, then Strife (and with it our world) appeared on top for a time before Love reasserted itself once more.

While it would be rather previous to suggest a direct link to the work of Charles Darwin, it's certainly true that Empedocles talked about the origins of living creatures in such a way as

to suggest some form of evolution. In his version of events, there was an initial period in which limbs wandered round on their own – calves with the faces of men, children with the heads of cattle, and other oddities – before more familiar territory was reached. He also came up with a theory explaining our awareness of things: particles of elements from other objects interact with our sense organs and enter through our pores, at which point they are detected by the corresponding particles in us.

In a second poem, *Purifications*, which may or may not be part of *On Nature* but certainly takes a more overtly religious line, Empedocles seems to have incorporated the ideas of Pythagoras and his followers on the transmigration of souls into his system. He describes the physical journey made by a soul in terms of an ongoing cycle: from a state of godlike innocence to a fall into mortality (as a result of shedding the blood of men and animals), followed by purification and deification once more, with Love and Strife again driving events.

Protagoras
(*c*. 490–420 BC)

Born in Abdera in north-eastern Greece, Protagoras travelled regularly to Athens and other cities, pursuing his career as a teacher. It was in Athens that he met Pericles, who invited him to write the legal code for the new Athenian colony of Thurii in

Italy – a pretty good vindication of his views on justice and virtue, which we'll come to shortly. Protagoras was possibly the first of a growing number of intellectuals known as sophists (from *sophos*, 'wise'), who expounded on a range of philosophical and practical subjects, and were held in such esteem that their students paid for the privilege of listening to them. He taught rhetoric, which was a fundamental requirement for anyone intending to take part in public life in ancient Greece, and also poetry, grammar and syntax. According to Plato's *Protagoras*, he claimed he could teach virtue, too.

Protagoras is best known for his relativism and his agnosticism. With his assertion that 'Man is the measure of all things, of the existence of the things that are and the non-existence of the things that are not', he was signalling his belief that there were no fixed, objective standards – Parmenides, eat your heart out – but rather that things varied with the individual and with circumstances. So while I might well feel hot on a summer's day in northern Europe, someone used to living in the Sahara would most likely find it rather nippy. Protagoras took this approach a step further, pointing out that it was equally applicable to matters of beauty, virtue, truth and justice; essentially, it's all relative.

Protagoras presumably saw this relativism in a positive light, as a break from the constraints of existing philosophy and religion, opening the way for democratic debate. However, he was later criticized for allowing more unscrupulous people to play with words, making 'the worse case appear better' – which explains today's negative connotations of 'sophistry', using clever-clever arguments without ethical constraints. Still,

Protagoras himself and the so-called Older Sophists were known as honest men who respected the law. As to the gods, Protagoras said he had no way of knowing whether they existed or not, or what form they might take, the subject being too obscure and life too short.

With his emphasis on the importance of subjectivity in how we understand the universe, Protagoras started the shift away from natural philosophy towards an interest in human values. And it was in response to Sophists like him that Plato began his search for transcendent, eternal truths that underpinned the human experience.

THE GREEK HEAVYWEIGHTS

Ask most people with the slightest interest in the subject to name you a philosopher and they will probably come up with one of the Big Three: Socrates, Plato and Aristotle. These are the names that have lasted down the centuries – these are the boys with the bright ideas. They mark, once and for all, the shift away from natural philosophy – all those books and poems entitled *On Nature* – towards the personal, with an emphasis on the use of reason in order to achieve wisdom and virtue, from which personal happiness (and, by extension on the wider stage, political well-being) can flow. It's presumably no coincidence that they were all based in Athens for long periods, at a time when the city was the intellectual and political centre of the classical world.

Towards the end of the fourth century BC, with the overshadowing of Athens and the other Greek city-states after the military exploits of King Philip II of Macedon and his son Alexander the Great, two new schools of philosophy, Epicureanism and Stoicism, fronted respectively by Epicurus and Zeno of Citium, came to the fore. They continued to exert influence throughout the Hellenistic period and into Roman times.

〰️

Socrates

(*c.* 470–399 BC)

WISE WORDS:

'The unexamined life is not worth living.'

– Quoted by Plato in his *Apology*

Born in Athens, Socrates left no written body of work, founded no school of philosophy and had no formal group of disciples, yet he is considered the first great figure of ancient philosophy. This is because he marks a clear break with earlier philosophical speculation about the origins and nature of the universe, turning instead to an analysis of ethics and the moral concepts by which human beings should live.

What little information we have about Socrates comes from three very different sources: the comic playwright Aristophanes, the military commander Xenophon and the great philosopher Plato, who was a student of Socrates. Each of them obviously had his own angle. Aristophanes portrays Socrates as a buffoon in his play *The Clouds*, while for Xenophon he was a soldier and a man of action. It is largely thanks to Plato that we know about Socrates' philosophical views. Plato outlines these in the form of dialogues, using this dramatic approach to convey both the method (dialectical reasoning) and the beliefs (the pursuit of moral good) of his master. It is thought that the *Apology* (the defence speech at Socrates' trial), *Crito* and *Phaedo* most accurately reflect Socrates' teachings.

The dialogues are presented as lengthy question-and-answer sessions with a range of people – politicians, students and friends – and explore widely held attitudes towards such fundamental concepts, or 'virtues', as justice, courage, moderation, wisdom and piety. According to Plato, Socrates always claimed that he himself knew nothing. Rather than imposing his own views on others, he challenged people to defend the logical basis for their ideas, the theory being that this would force them to confront contradictions in their own arguments. Only then, when false logic had been stripped away by a process of elimination, would people accept their ignorance and seek universally applicable definitions for the virtues fundamental to human life, in the process revealing a deeper moral good.

For Socrates, righteous living was the key. This included resisting the pursuit of fame and fortune and never, under any circumstances, returning evil for evil. The most important thing in life was to look after the moral welfare of one's soul, as this was the route to true happiness. It was a very personal philosophy: once the meaning of the virtues had been clarified and understood, one could become an objectively better person, unswayed by ties to family and friends.

Unfortunately for Socrates, his constant challenging of widely held beliefs eventually put him at odds with the state; he was brought to trial in 399 BC, and charged with introducing new gods and corrupting the youth. Whatever the validity of the charges, these were politically turbulent times. The famed

Athenian democracy had only been restored in 401 BC, after a period of over thirty years that had seen humiliating defeat by Sparta in the Peloponnesian War and the imposition of rule by the Spartan-backed 'Thirty Tyrants', who murdered so many Athenian citizens that they lasted in power for just a year. Perhaps understandably, the city's new leaders were not too kindly disposed towards someone who seemed to take such delight in pointing out where they were going wrong, especially as that someone had formerly been the teacher of one of the leading tyrants.

When it came to his trial, Socrates was not to be deflected from his objective intellectual stance. He was given the option of paying a fine instead of facing the death sentence, but turned it down; he was then offered the chance to escape from prison through bribery, but rejected it. His reasoning was that, no matter what the outcome, a citizen should always obey the laws of the state. And so, having lived uncompromisingly for philosophy, in the end he drank hemlock and died for it.

THE ACADEMY AWARDS

Plato set up his school for philosophers in a grove dedicated to the hero Akademos, which explains why it came to be known as the Academy, which in turn explains why scholarly types are known as academics.

◎◎

Plato

(427–347 BC)

WISE WORDS:

'Philosophy begins in wonder.'

— *Theaetetus*

Born in Athens into an aristocratic family, Plato seems to have been destined for a life in politics before he became a student of Socrates, about whose trial and subsequent death he later wrote. Disillusioned by these events, Plato left Athens in 399 BC and travelled in Greece and Egypt, southern Italy and Sicily. By around 387 BC he was back in Athens, however, and it is here that he established the Academy, which some have called the first university. It was a place for philosophical, mathematical and scientific study with the aim of improving political life in Greek cities, and Plato presided over it for the rest of his life. Most of his works have come down to us in the form of conversations, referred to as dialogues, between Socrates and a range of other people. Since Plato himself never features, we can quite safely assume that he shared the opinions of his teacher.

In the early dialogues, Socrates attempts to tease out definitions of moral virtues by grilling individuals about their beliefs: so, for example, he discusses piety with Euthyphro, an expert on religion, and courage with Laches, a general, in the dialogues that bear their names. And he goes at his task in such a rigorous, relentless way that their initially confident assertions are dismantled step by step, revealed as being riddled with inconsistencies, and everyone, Socrates included, ends up bamboozled. Which might have been a satisfying intellectual exercise for Socrates, but no doubt drove everyone else mad.

The middle dialogues – among them *Phaedo* (a discussion of Socrates' death, which leads on to talk of immortality) and *The Republic* (considerations of justice as regards the individual and the state) – display a more positive, constructive approach. Here Plato outlines a number of important ideas: that the soul is immortal and consists of three parts (one that seeks to satisfy basic appetites, one that responds to active qualities such as courage, and one that is represented by the intellect); that knowledge is actually recollection of a time before our immortal soul was imprisoned in our body; and that the changing material world of objects (pale shadows we recognize only by perception, opinion or belief) masks the eternal reality of forms, which exist beyond most people's understanding. Perfect and ideal, these forms are the ultimate goal of knowledge.

The famous allegory of the cave is to be found in *The Republic*. Here Socrates (via Plato) describes humans as prisoners who have been chained all their life in a cave, able to perceive the world only via shadows cast on the wall in front of them by the light of a fire behind them. In other words, they see shadows rather than reality; indeed, the shadows *are* their reality. The philosopher's role in society is to leave the cave and finally see the world for what it is.

As for the soul, again, the philosopher will be able to keep all three parts in harmony, not allowing any one to dominate. And the same can be said of society, for Plato equates the three parts of

the soul with the three classes of society: rulers, soldiers and the common people. For there to be a just society, each class must keep to its own sphere, with the ruler immersing himself in philosophy to aid him in his task – though when Plato twice attempted to put his theories into practice in Syracuse in the 360s BC, instructing Dionysius II on how to become a philosopher-king, he became entangled in a political feud and was soon back in Athens.

The later dialogues backtrack on the business of forms and instead delve more deeply into concepts of knowledge, revisit the ideal republic and explore the natural world via physics and chemistry, physiology and medicine.

Plato's Academy continued to exist until AD 529, when it was closed by the Emperor Justinian in an attempt to suppress pagan Hellenistic culture, but his ideas did not disappear. Plato is certainly still seen as the person who introduced the philosophical argument as we think of it today, while the range and depth of his interests have never been surpassed. As Alfred North Whitehead pointed out in *Process and Reality*, 'The safest general characterization of the European philosophical tradition is that it consists of a series of footnotes to Plato.'

SO WHAT'S PLATONIC LOVE, THEN?

As most people know, a platonic relationship is one that's affectionate, intimate even, but stops short of sex. What not so many people know is that this definition harks back to Plato and his doctrine of 'forms'. Beyond the sexual desire that is constantly throbbing through the material world, demanding immediate satisfaction, lies the idealized form of beauty that true love aspires to. Allegedly ...

Aristotle

(384–322 BC)

WISE WORDS:

'Human good turns out to be the active exercise of the soul in conformity with excellence or virtue ... But this activity must take place throughout a complete lifetime, for one swallow does not make a summer, any more than one fine day.'

— *Nicomachean Ethics*

The son of a doctor – in fact, *the* doctor at the court of the increasingly powerful kings of Macedon – Aristotle was born in Stagira in northern Greece. In 367 BC, he went to Athens, where

HAS ANYONE EVER TOLD YOU THAT YOU'RE A CYNIC?

If so, they no doubt meant that you are the sort of person who believes others are motivated purely by self-interest. What they might not have known is that they were also referring to the school of philosophy particularly associated with Diogenes of Sinope (*c.* 410–*c.* 325 BC).

The Cynics favoured an extreme form of asceticism and self-sufficiency, believing that morality (and therefore happiness) depended on abandoning the trappings of civilization and returning to the simplicity of nature. Diogenes was legendary for his lack of interest in social niceties and creature comforts, preferring to live in a tub rather than a house. When asked why he walked through Athens carrying a lantern in broad daylight, he claimed to be looking for an honest man. According to another story, when Alexander the Great asked Diogenes what he would like, the philosopher replied, 'You to move out of the sun and not cast a shadow on me.' In other words, he wasn't interested in the outer trappings of success. Instead, his life was devoted to undermining the artificial values and institutions of a society he considered morally bankrupt.

he was initially a pupil and then became a teacher at Plato's Academy. He left after twenty years, possibly miffed at not being chosen to replace Plato when the great man died, and, among other things, spent time tutoring the young Alexander (who was not yet Great). He returned to Athens in 335 BC and established his own school, which was called the Lyceum because it was near the site where Apollo Lycaeus, the god Apollo in a wolf incarnation, was honoured. Here Aristotle taught for the next twelve years, but he had to leave on the death of Alexander (now Great) in 323 BC, as a wave of anti-Macedonian sentiment swept through Athens, carrying him along with it.

The majority of Aristotle's work survived in the form of treatises or lecture notes. He seems to have had something to say on virtually every subject under the sun: logic, metaphysics, ethics, politics, rhetoric, poetry, literary analysis, meteorology, astronomy, biology, zoology, physics and psychology. These notes would have been intended for serious students originally, not for general consumption, but they were collected together in the first century BC by Andronicus of Rhodes, at which point they would no doubt have been edited. This does mean that the first published versions of Aristotle's work, not to mention the subsequent Latin and Arabic translations, were based on someone else's interpretation, but no matter. The result is that his *Organon* (on logic), *Metaphysics*, *Nicomachean Ethics*, *Politics*, *On Rhetoric*, *Poetics* and plenty of others can still be read today.

Aristotle effectively established the science of logic, refining universal rules of reasoning to help in the pursuit of knowledge. Take this one of his as an example:

step 1 All men are mortal.

step 2 Socrates is a man.

step 3 Therefore Socrates is mortal.

That's a classic bit of syllogism, that is, using deductive inference. Or, to put it more simply: if steps 1 and 2 are true, you can deduce step 3.

Then there's his work on metaphysics – the search for first principles. Everything that exists can be assigned to a category: so it's a substance or a quality or a quantity or a … (Aristotle lists as many as ten categories sometimes). There's a hierarchy here: to stick with Socrates, the fact that he's a man (see above) means that he belongs in substance; his personal qualities cannot precede his substance. Meanwhile, substance itself is made up of matter (the physical component parts) and form (structure, which is normally determined by function). This is not 'form' in Plato's sense of an idealized version that exists elsewhere, but something grounded in the here and now – the universal essence of whatever the object in question. Aristotle then identifies four causes of everything: the material cause (what something's made of); the formal cause (what it actually is); the efficient cause (its means of creation); and the final cause (its purpose).

As for ethics, Aristotle points out that, although everyone seeks the good life, 'good' is not one particular quality. Before a man can be considered good, he has first to determine what his function is; only then, when he has performed his function well, will he achieve his goal. Since the function of man – the thing he can do that no other object can – is to reason, and by extension control his desires and conduct *through* reason, there is an ethical or moral side to his search. Virtue is a matter of finding the right balance – the so-called golden mean – between opposing vices.

We could continue, but the value of Aristotle's contribution across the vast range of subjects he considered goes way beyond the doctrines he espoused and the conclusions he reached. It was his clear-sighted, skilful analysis of arguments that made him such an important figure, and it is little wonder that his influence extended through medieval Christian (see Thomas Aquinas, p.78) and Islamic (see Averroes, p.72) philosophy into the modern world.

Epicurus
(341–270 BC)

Born to Athenian parents on the island of Samos, Epicurus spent some time teaching in Asia Minor before eventually settling in Athens around 307 BC. He set up a school known as the Garden, which was – obviously – in his garden, where he taught for the rest of his life. Although only fragments of his work survive, his opinions have come down to us through the writings of his followers, most notably the Roman poet and philosopher Lucretius in his *De rerum natura* (*The Nature of Things*).

Known as a hedonist (from the Greek *hēdonē*, 'pleasure'), Epicurus held that pleasure is the greatest good, is always good

CAN YOU CALL EPICURUS A HEDONIST TODAY? OR EVEN AN EPICUREAN?

On the one hand yes, but on the other no. Hedonism is the ethical doctrine proposing the pursuit of pleasure as the aim of life and is certainly linked with Epicurus. Indeed, according to the Roman philosopher and statesman Seneca (see p.49), a sign at the entrance to Epicurus' school read, 'Stranger, here you will do well to tarry; here our highest good is pleasure'. So far so good …

But of course it all depends on what you mean by pleasure. Somehow you can't help thinking that the aims of a modern hedonist might well differ from those of the followers of Epicurus, for whom pleasure was not a fortnight's drug-fuelled clubbing in Ibiza but a state of tranquillity achieved through the absence of pain and anxiety.

As to being an epicurean, again, it's all in the name. Today an epicure is someone with a pronounced interest in fine food and wine. Pleasurable, sure, but not in the way that the great man – who was remarkably abstemious – intended.

and is to be achieved by avoiding pain. Where pleasure concerns the body, perfect health is its highest form; where it concerns the mind, freedom from fear and anxiety is the way forward. Although all pleasure is good, some pleasure will inevitably bring with it pain, and this is where wisdom comes into play – wisdom allows people to make the best choice of pleasures.

Epicurus went on to adapt atomism, the theory that everything in the universe is made up of minute particles moving in empty space that was put forward by an earlier philosopher, Democritus. Where Democritus had his atoms coming down in parallel lines, rather like rain, but colliding every so often in a predetermined sort of way to cause things to change, Epicurus suggested that atoms could swerve for no apparent reason – or rather, that they had free will. He was also a committed empiricist, teaching that all knowledge is ultimately grounded in observation and deduction.

These teachings fed into each other. Once there was no predetermined course of events, no gods controlling what went on in people's lives, one potential cause of anxiety had gone. Nor should anyone worry about death, since that was the end of consciousness and so would not be felt. Instead, Epicurus set great store by friendship, seeing it as a major ingredient of happiness, and praised simple pleasures – food and shelter – over wealth and political power. All of which makes it odd to think that modern definitions of hedonists and epicureans have strayed so far from their original meanings (see p.43).

THE STOICS

It's not a paradox this time … there really was another Zeno. In his early twenties, Zeno of Citium (*c.* 333–262 BC) came to Athens, where he studied for a time at the Academy. He eventually went on to teach at the Stoa Poikilē ('Painted Colonnade' – this particular *stoa* was in the Agora, the main marketplace), which gave its name to his brand of philosophy, Stoicism.

No doubt in response to the prevailing political instability – by the end of the fourth century BC, the Greek city-states were in decline, which led to both personal

insecurity and a more general sense of moral disintegration – the Stoics were, in the modern sense of the word, all for remaining stoical: indifferent to pleasure and pain, to the ups and downs of fortune. Specifically, they believed that the only thing completely within an individual's control was the ability to acquire the correct moral attitude, which could be equated with virtue and was grounded in knowledge. For the Stoics, happiness came from knowing the right thing to do in any given circumstance at any given time. Chasing after success was nothing but an irrelevance.

The ideas of the Stoics were taken up and developed over the years, coming to prominence again most notably in Roman times (see Seneca, p.49, and Marcus Aurelius, p.55).

ENTER THE ROMANS

◎◎

A thens was sidelined politically after defeat by Philip II of
Macedon in 338 BC. With the military exploits of his son
Alexander the Great – in twelve short years he overwhelmed the
Persian Empire, his armies reaching as far as the Russian
steppes, Afghanistan and the Punjab – the balance of power
shifted not only within Greece but also to areas beyond.

After Alexander's death in 323 BC, his conquests were eventually – and acrimoniously – divided between his successors,
Antigonus, Ptolemy and Seleucus. They effectively oversaw the
creation of the Hellenistic world from their kingdoms in
Macedon, Egypt and the vast eastern part of the empire, spreading Greek culture far and wide. But Athens still remained the
centre for anyone interested in philosophical studies.

It was against this background that some new thinkers began
to make their presence felt. Just as Alexander was setting off on
his travels, Rome was beginning to stir; by the middle of the third
century BC, it had gained control of all Italy south of the River Po.
From there, it extended its interests into Sicily, Corsica and
Sardinia, and the rest of the Mediterranean began to look increasingly tempting. By around 200 BC, the Romans had arguably

established a culture of their own, with political systems in place that would develop into the full-blown Roman Republic.

Initially, any Roman wishing to study philosophy headed to Athens, where the various schools of philosophy continued to operate. That situation came to an end in 87 BC, when the Roman statesman and general Sulla besieged and then sacked Athens. The city was ruined and a number of its philosophers left, taking their philosophical texts to other centres in the Mediterranean world, including Rome.

There were no exclusively Roman schools of philosophy, which remained a Greek import. Indeed, prior to Lucretius' *De rerum natura* (see Epicurus, p.42), there was no philosophical work written in Latin, and Lucretius himself spoke of the difficulty of

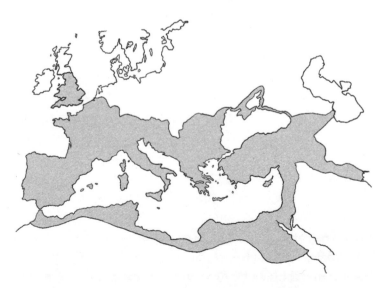

The Roman Empire at its greatest extent, early second century AD

finding Latin words subtle enough to express the finer points of Epicurean physics. But pre-existing schools of philosophy, in particular Epicureanism and Stoicism, influenced many spheres of Roman life. They contributed to higher education with their emphasis on rhetoric and grammar, and to religion with their analyses of ethics and spirituality. And when the civil wars brought the Republic to a close in 27 BC and ushered in the first of the Roman emperors, they even provided a framework to help Republican senators bear their loss of power. So influential was Stoic thought – and obviously also adaptable to a range of political situations – that, by the middle of the first century AD, one of its keenest exponents was tutoring the future emperor Nero, while in the second century it could claim a Roman emperor all for itself (see Marcus Aurelius, p.55).

Seneca

(4 BC–AD 65)

WISE WORDS:

'That man lives badly who does not know how to die well.'
— *On Tranquillity of the Mind*

The Roman Stoic Lucius Annaeus Seneca (the Younger) was born in Cordoba, Spain, the son of a wealthy and well-connected rhetorician and historian. As a young man he studied philosophy and rhetoric in Rome, with a view to pursuing a career in politics.

He certainly seems to have made some worthwhile connections there, because by his thirties he was moving in imperial circles. But, as plenty of other people were to discover over the years, it was virtually impossible to remain unscathed by court intrigues.

Having found favour during the reign of Caligula, Seneca was then banished in AD 41, accused of committing adultery with Julia, Caligula's sister (and the new emperor Claudius' niece), who by all accounts was something of a wild child. He spent the next eight years in Corsica, before being recalled to Rome to act as tutor to the young Nero. When Nero became emperor in 54, Seneca initially retained his influence, even becoming consul three years later – and amassing a considerable fortune in the process. But in the end the notoriously unstable emperor took against him and Seneca withdrew from public life in 62. Alas, that didn't stop Nero from ordering his suicide three years later, of which more in a moment.

Seneca's philosophy is conveyed through his *Moral Essays* and *Moral Epistles to Lucilius*, a series of ten dialogues and 124 letters in Latin in which he gives practical advice on a range of subjects: providence, friendship, the brevity of life, the terrors of death, groundless fears, anger, virtue, the happy life, benefits, clemency, the simple life, tranquillity and so on. Among them are his famous *Consolations*, notably one to his mother, Helvia, on his exile to Corsica and another to a woman named Marcia on the death of her sons; both attempt to show how reason can help someone to bear unhappiness with courage. Throughout all these works, self-control is of paramount importance. For Seneca, no one can be considered great until they have learned to master themselves and to moderate their desires. Suffering is merely a test that will strengthen an individual, while anger, grief and fear are emotional traps that will enslave them.

Some have suggested that Seneca's Stoicism arose from his struggles to cope with the events that befell him, rather than from considered philosophical conviction. It's true that there are contradictions between Seneca the politician and Seneca the Stoic philosopher, the wealthy man at home with emperors who championed the virtues of self-control and the simple life. But his was an attempt to apply philosophy in a practical way, and as tutor to an emperor he was in a better position than most to try to put his ideas into practice.

Either way, if his life was contradictory, he certainly died in a brave and dignified – not to mention horribly drawn-out – fashion. Having received Nero's order to commit suicide, he slit the veins in his arm with a dagger; when that didn't do the trick, he drank poison; finally, running out of options, he had his servants place him in a bath of boiling water, where he suffocated in the steam.

'SENECA CANNOT BE TOO HEAVY ...'

So says Polonius in Shakespeare's *Hamlet*, when talking about the itinerant actors who have conveniently shown up at Elsinore, and demonstrating in the process that Elizabethan audiences knew Seneca as a playwright. In addition to his philosophical works, Seneca wrote eight big, bloated, gory tragedies:

Hercules Furens, *The Trojan Women*, *The Phoenician Women*, *Medea*, *Phaedra*, *Agamemnon*, *Thyestes* and *Oedipus*. These were adapted from originals by Euripides, Aeschylus and Sophocles, but where the Greek playwrights left violence in the background, Seneca brought it to the fore, with generous side orders of revenge and the supernatural, leaving his stage littered with corpses at the end. Remind you of Shakespeare at all? Sadly, for Seneca's contemporaries, it would probably have been all too reminiscent of life at Nero's court.

Epictetus

(55–135)

WISE WORDS:

'But what is philosophy? Does it not mean making preparation to meet the things that come upon us?'

— *Discourses*

Born a slave in Hieropolis, Phrygia (part of Turkey now), Epictetus went with his master to Rome, where he studied under the Stoic teacher Musonius Rufus. At some point he gained his freedom and began to teach, but in 89 he and other philosophers were banished from Rome by the Emperor Domitian. Epictetus chose to settle in Nicopolis in north-western Greece, where he opened his own highly successful school.

Among his students was the future historian Arrian, who collected Epictetus' comments on the works of earlier Stoics into the *Discourses* and the *Handbook*. Written in Greek with a view to elucidating the philosophical way of life, the *Discourses* – there were originally eight books, but only four survive – range over such topics as friendship, illness, fear, poverty, acquiring and maintaining tranquillity and why it is wrong to be angry with others. The *Handbook* is a manual of Stoic ethics, illustrated by everyday examples.

In both works, Epictetus teaches that the purpose of philosophy is to enable the individual to lead a better life, to live virtuously according to nature and with an awareness of responsibilities to others, and thus to achieve happiness. The starting point must be self-examination, with an assessment of which things in life can be controlled and which cannot, since unhappiness is caused by worrying about things over which we have no power. So our opinions are our own – likes and dislikes, judgements and so on – but such things as health, wealth and all forms of public acclaim are beyond our control. The choice is between the freedom that follows when an individual exercises *moral* will and the slavery that results from being misled by the external trappings of success. With discipline and self-knowledge, the twin goals of imperturbability (*ataraxia*) and freedom from passion (*apatheia*) in the face of life's upsets will be achieved and, in the words of the *Handbook*, 'no one will ever put compulsion or hindrance on you, you will blame none, you will accuse none, you will do nothing against your will, no one will harm you, you will have no enemy, for no harm can touch you'.

Epictetus' brand of practical Stoicism was addressed not to the ruling elite – even though the Emperor Hadrian apparently attended his lectures on occasion – but to a much wider audience, the ordinary people. And they would presumably have found it pretty reassuring at a time when, on the political front, it was becoming increasingly clear that they had little or no power to stand against the might of the imperial machine.

'TO HIMSELF'

Meditations was not a title used by Marcus Aurelius. In fact, these pieces were not written for or seen by his contemporaries. They first appeared in book form in 1558, published by Andreas Gesner of Zurich, with a Latin translation by Wilhelm Xylander. The original manuscript from which they worked had been in the library of Otto Heinrich, the Elector Palatine, and is now lost. Apparently it bore the inscription *'ta eis heauton'* ('to himself'), which accurately conveys the fact that Marcus Aurelius was recording private, intimate reflections rather than writing for other people.

Marcus Aurelius

(121–80)

WISE WORDS:

'Consider that everything which happens, happens justly, and if thou observest carefully, thou wilt find it to be so.'

— Meditations

A favourite of the Emperor Hadrian, Marcus Aurelius was educated by a number of the best teachers in Rome, including the orator Fronto (letters between them survive), and from a young age showed a keen interest in philosophy, especially the works of Epictetus. He was adopted in 138 by Antoninus Pius, who succeeded Hadrian as emperor that year, and then made consul in 140 and again in 145. He carried out his public duties conscientiously while still pursuing his studies in philosophy and law, and became emperor in 161.

Throughout his reign, Marcus Aurelius had to deal with a number of military threats in the northern and eastern parts of the empire. There was trouble in Britain, along the Rhine and along the Danube to the north, while in the east the Parthians invaded Armenia and Syria. To make matters worse, plague broke out among the eastern armies and then in Rome. While he was off contending with these problems between 170 and 180, the emperor recorded his thoughts on a range of topics from whichever military camp he was based at. Eventually, what must have started as a private journal written in Greek became the twelve books of the *Meditations*.

The *Meditations* serve as a sort of Stoic self-help manual. For Marcus Aurelius the ultimate aim in life is to live in harmony with the universe, of which all people are a part and to which they will all return. The way to achieve this is to ignore the distraction of worldly pleasures and aspire instead to self-control, which comes with the use of reason. More important than what people *are* is the way they behave, and they can train themselves to behave better by following Stoic principles. Among the qualities the emperor considers worthy are restraint, simplicity, steadfastness, self-control, submitting to providence, the ability to control anger, and indifference to what cannot be altered.

Writing in 1503, Machiavelli (see p.85) named Marcus Aurelius as the last of the 'Five Good Emperors', praising him for having led a good life and demonstrated such devotion to duty. From the emperor's point of view, his interpretation of Stoic philosophy, with its emphasis on accepting responsibilities, exercising self-control and enduring whatever comes along, must have been particularly comforting during times of war and plague.

ATHENS BACK IN VOGUE AGAIN

With his great interest in philosophy, not to mention his clout as master of the universe, the Emperor Marcus Aurelius established four chairs of philosophy in Athens in 177. There was one for each of the main schools – Platonic, Aristotelian, Stoic and Epicurean – and they were endowed with nice fat salaries, too.

Plotinus

(c. 205–70)

Born in Egypt, Plotinus studied philosophy in Alexandria for eleven years before joining the Emperor Gordian's expedition against the Persians in 243. He hoped, by doing so, to learn something about Persian and Indian philosophy, but when Gordian was murdered in Mesopotamia he abandoned his plans and escaped to Antioch (in present-day Turkey). He then made his way to Rome, arriving in 244, and spent most of the rest of his life there teaching philosophy, leaving only shortly before he died.

In 253, Plotinus started writing the treatises that would be collected together after his death by his pupil Porphyry and published in about 300 as the *Enneads* (from the Greek *ennea*, 'nine', because each of the six books contained nine treatises). These laid the foundations of Neoplatonism, which synthesized the earlier philosophical teachings of Aristotle, the Pythagoreans and the Stoics with those of Plato. Like Plato, Plotinus insists that the intellect is superior to the senses, and the spiritual world to the material. His universe can be divided into a hierarchy of realities, at the top of which is the 'One'. Transcendental, perfect and complete in itself, the One – which equates with the 'Good' in Plato's *Republic* – has no attributes or component parts. It is simply supreme goodness, and it emanates like light from the sun, or indeed overflows, to form the next world down: Intellect. Conceived by the mind of the One, this is the world of ideas and concepts – they equate with Plato's 'forms' – and it in turn overflows into the world of Soul, which is eternal but actively creates and orders the visible universe. From Soul we descend to Nature, peopled with individual souls, and then to the material world, which is the weakest of realities, no longer capable of emanation. Each individual has within him elements of matter, nature, soul and intellect, and must aspire, through contemplation and self-discipline, to reach back up through the hierarchy.

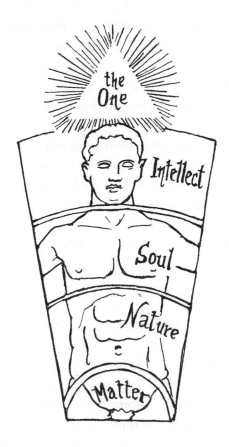

Plotinus himself claimed to have experienced the ecstasy that came following union with the One.

With its fusion of the works of earlier thinkers, Plotinus' Neoplatonism can be seen as the last major contribution to classical philosophy. At the same time, its emphasis on contemplation as a means for lowly humans to commune directly with the One, who sounds remarkably like God, exerted considerable influence on early Christian theology, especially the work of St Augustine, thus creating a bridge between the ancient and medieval worlds.

NEUPLATONISCH?

The term Neoplatonism is not one that would have been recognized in the ancient world. It seems to have come into use in Germany in the mid-nineteenth century, when academics decreed that there was enough new thinking among Plotinus and his followers – who would have considered themselves Platonists – to warrant some sort of distinction.

CHRISTIANS, MUSLIMS AND JUST ONE JEW

◎◎

It must have been pretty obvious that all was not well in the Roman world when, in 308, there were no fewer than six emperors at the same time, three in the east and three in the west. Sooner rather than later, the vast and unwieldy empire was going to split in two. After a fair bit of jostling, the struggle for power in the west came down to a fight between Maxentius and Constantine, who faced each other for the last time at the Milvian Bridge, near Rome, in 312. Here, Constantine was victorious against his rival's superior forces, and, according to legend, he had divine help.

In his *Life of Constantine*, Eusebius – known as the Father of Church History, he became Bishop of Caesarea in Palestine at about the time of the battle – describes how, the night before his great victory, Constantine saw a flaming cross inscribed with the words 'In this sign, you will conquer'. The sign was the Chi-Rho, the intertwined Greek letters that form the opening of Christ's name. Other writers tell different versions of the story, but everyone is agreed that Constantine promptly converted to Christianity. Then, the following year, he and Licinius, who was now emperor in the east, issued the Edict of Milan, which extended religious tolerance to Christians throughout the empire. Obviously Christians had been around for a good while, but this was the first time they'd been given official backing. So no more being thrown to the lions …

Fast-forward 300 years or so and another empire, based on another religion, was about to appear on the scene. The prophet Muhammad, founder of Islam, was born in Mecca around

570. At the age of forty, having spent much time in religious contemplation, he began preaching the new faith, based on the Qur'an, which had been revealed to him by Allah, the all-powerful, just and compassionate God. Muhammad spoke out against idolatry and superstition, exhorting people to lead a better life through prayer, fasting and almsgiving. He must have been seen as too much of a troublemaker by the authorities, however, because eventually the Meccans rose up against him and his followers. In 622 – the date of the Hegira (literally 'departure'), which counts as year 1 for Muslims – they fled to Medina, where Muhammad became the chief judge and ruler of the city. From there he embarked on a war against the enemies of Islam, and in 630 he captured Mecca. This time he was recognized as a ruler and prophet of the new religion, which then began to take hold across Arabia. Muhammad fell ill shortly after returning from his last pilgrimage to Mecca in 632, and died the same year.

His immediate successors, the four Rashidun Caliphs, oversaw a period of military expansion during which Islam was introduced into vast swathes of land that had previously been part of the Roman and Persian empires, with all the ensuing cultural overlap. The Umayyad Caliphs, who came next, continued the expansion through North Africa and into Spain from their capital in Damascus. The following dynasty, the Abbasids, moved the capital from Damascus to the newly founded city of Baghdad, from where they tried to retain control of their rapidly expanding empire from the middle of the eighth century until their eventual conquest by the Mongols in the thirteenth century.

During the heyday of the Abbasids, Baghdad became an intellectual hotbed, home to Muslim and non-Muslim scholars alike. They oversaw, among other things, the translation into Arabic of works on philosophy, science, medicine and education from the classical world that would otherwise have been lost. Rival Muslim dynasties established themselves throughout the empire and they also fostered scholarship and intellectual enquiry. Notably Cairo in Egypt under the Fatimids and Cordoba in Andalusia under the Umayyads became important centres where, in a spirit of tolerance that embraced Christians and Jews, great thinkers from different religious backgrounds were able to flourish.

In the early days of Muslim expansion, Christian Western Europe was in the doldrums. Even if the Dark Ages weren't quite as dark as people have made out, there doesn't seem to have been a lot happening on the intellectual front. But in the twelfth century, those classical works that had been translated into Arabic in Baghdad and other Islamic centres, most notably the works of Aristotle, began to make their way back again, retranslated into Hebrew, Greek and Latin, to become available in the West once more.

So, by the Middle Ages, the three great monotheistic religions – Judaism, Christianity and Islam – had all come into contact with Greek philosophy. In each case, the works of Aristotle were the main point of reference, but there was also an interest in Neoplatonism, which both influenced interpretations of Aristotle and staked its own claim for attention. Because what the different religious thinkers wanted to do next was apply the thoughts of the ancient philosophers to their own particular theologies.

THE SECOND MASTER

This was the title given to al-Farabi (*c.* 870–950), the earliest of the Islamic religious philosophers, or *falasifa* as they were known in Arabic. The title of one of his works, *The Harmonization of the Opinions of the Two Sages the Divine Plato and Aristotle*, makes his intentions clear. His idea was to come up with a synthesis that incorporated the mystical 'One' of Plotinus and the Neoplatonists and the logic and empiricism of Aristotle – the First Master – and then apply it to theology. His approach was hugely influential for later Muslim, Christian and Jewish philosophers.

☙☙

St Augustine of Hippo

(354–430)

WISE WORDS:

'Grant me chastity and continence, but not yet.'

– Confessions

Born in North Africa to a Christian mother and a pagan father, Augustine can be seen as a bridge between classical and Christian philosophy, though to begin with he had little to do with

Christianity. As a young man, he taught rhetoric in Carthage, which was a thriving intellectual centre. While living there he had a son by his mistress and became involved with Manichaeism – a religious belief system centred on the constant struggle between light and dark/good and evil. Scepticism took his fancy next, followed by Neoplatonism, which was something he became very interested in while teaching in Rome and then Milan. It was in Milan in 387 that he converted to Christianity. He was baptized the following year, ordained a priest in 391, and in 396 became the bishop of Hippo (now in Algeria).

Augustine was a prolific author and his major works, *The Confessions* and *The City of God*, are still read today. For him, philosophy and theology were inextricably linked. Once he converted, Christianity became the true philosophy for him, while the pagan beliefs and schools of philosophy he had previously favoured were treated as less well-developed theologies – resources to help him elucidate the Christian message.

From Plato and the Neoplatonists Augustine took the idea that there is a distinction between the imperfect, transient world of material things, accessed via the senses, and the perfect, eternal world, accessed via the intellect: the City of Men vs. the City of God. This distinction is part of a larger, interlocking hierarchy that starts with absolute unity and then works down through levels of increasing materiality. And absolute unity is God, the ultimate source for all that comes after. Synonymous with Being, Goodness and Truth, God is the fixed point that unifies everything within an eternal, rational hierarchy and it is to God that individuals must open their minds in order to achieve wisdom and enlightenment.

So how to explain evil in a divinely ordained world? The Manichaean dualist approach was no answer, because God is unity. Instead, original sin is to blame. The divine exists within us, but has been tarnished by what happened in the Garden of Eden. However, there is a remedy to hand: divine grace. The elect – God's chosen – were predestined to be saved from fiery damnation. This did not detract from individuals' free will to determine their own actions, but God, being present throughout time, the spiritual world being eternal, already knew how they would jump, and so had taken this into account before electing.

Basically, faith came first with Augustine, as the starting point from which to seek wisdom. By training to be a teacher, he moved from teaching rhetoric to teaching Christianity, using his own life as an illustration and applying his rigorous intellect to a wide range of doctrinal points that seemed to him to need clarification.

WHERE ON EARTH?

Where, in the *Republic*, Plato outlined an ideal state ruled by philosopher-kings, al-Farabi talked of prophet-imams and saw Medina as the perfect city, ruled by Muhammad. For St Augustine, the City of God was a spiritual rather than a geographical place, but the Church was its equivalent on earth.

THE FLOATING MAN

Avicenna asks you to imagine that a fully grown man suddenly comes into being floating in mid-air, blind-folded and limbs splayed. He can see nothing; he is touching nothing. But even without sensation he is aware of his own existence. An early version of 'I think, therefore I am'?

Avicenna

(980–1037)

The foremost physician and philosopher of his day – not to mention child prodigy (he could recite the Qur'an from memory before the age of ten) and all-round top scholar (he wrote on logic, chemistry, physics, geology, psychology, metaphysics and astronomy, to name but a few) – Ibn Sina is better known in the West by the Latin version of his name, Avicenna. He was born near Bukhara (in modern-day Uzbekistan), where he was educated, and, according to his modest autobiography, he had learned all there was to learn by the age of eighteen. He specifically mentions having wrestled with Aristotle's *Metaphysics* for a year and a half, reading it forty times before being satisfied that he fully understood the meaning, thanks to an al-Farabi commentary.

Avicenna's interest in applying Aristotelian and Neoplatonic ideas to Islamic theology is most fully expressed in his major philosophical work *The Book of Healing*, which covers logic, the natural sciences and metaphysics. Here he talks about the distinction between necessary and contingent being, or, in other words, between essence, which just *is*, and existence, which is a bit of a hit-and-miss affair – or, put another way, between what something *is* and the form it happens to take. For the essence of anything that exists to take physical form, there has to be a prior cause – something more powerful, whose own existence is higher in rank. There's a whole hierarchy of existent entities, but at the very top there must surely be something that wasn't caused by anything at all. This is the Necessary Being, in whom essence and existence are identical. In fact, this is God – self-existent and the cause of all other entities.

Avicenna went against traditional Muslim theologians in rejecting the idea that God created the world from nothing. He argues instead that the world has no beginning but follows on as a natural consequence of God's existence as the 'One', whose essence is knowledge, will and power. As the uncaused first cause, he is necessarily the creator. Logical or what?

∾∾

St Anselm

(1033–1109)

WISE WORDS:

'For this also I believe, that unless I believe, I shall not understand.'

– *Proslogion*

Born in Aosta, Anselm left Italy in 1056 to join the Benedictine abbey of Bec in Normandy, where he studied under Lanfranc, one of the pre-eminent Church scholars of his day. In 1093, he succeeded Lanfranc as Archbishop of Canterbury and on his death was buried in the cathedral.

Anselm can be seen as the first exponent of scholasticism, which was not so much a philosophy as an approach to learning that used dialectical reasoning to work through questions that arose, so as to resolve apparent contradictions in medieval theology. His aim was to reconcile reason with faith, for while reason was no substitute for faith, it could lead people to an understanding of what they had already accepted through faith.

Anselm is best known for his works setting out proofs for the existence of God. In the *Monologion*, he states that, in order to be able to call something good, there must necessarily be an objective standard: an absolute good against which we are judging. This absolute is what we call God. In the *Proslogion*, he goes further, coming up with his famous ontological argument (not that it was called that until much later): if God is agreed to be the absolute, a being greater than which no other can be conceived, then God must exist in reality, too, because otherwise it would be possible to conceive of another greater something.

It's one of those arguments that make more sense after a bottle of wine or two – and even in Anselm's day it was ridiculed by some scholars. However, over the years it has continued to be discussed by a range of philosophers, including Descartes, Leibniz and Kant (see pp.92, 102 and 118).

Averroes

(1126–98)

WISE WORDS:

'Since philosophy is true and the revealed scriptures are true, there can be no disharmony between them.'

– 'The Harmony of Religions and Philosophy'

The distinguished Islamic philosopher Averroes, or Ibn Rushd, was born in Cordoba into an important family of jurists. He too became a judge, first in his home town, then in Seville and finally in Marrakesh, where he died. He wrote on a range of subjects in addition to philosophy, including jurisprudence and medicine, and was at one time physician to the Caliph.

In the West, he is best known for his thirty-eight commentaries on the works of Aristotle and on Plato's *Republic*. Based on Arabic translations, some were straightforward summaries, but others included criticism of contributions from later commentators, not only the Neoplatonists but also al-Farabi and Avicenna (see pp.65 and 69). Averroes was intent on getting back to 'pure' Aristotelian thought, in part to undermine attacks from Islamic jurists and theologians that he felt were based on misreadings. He wanted to show that there was no conflict between religion and philosophy, that they were merely different ways to reach the same truth. Religious law (*sharia*), being based on faith, could and therefore should not be tested; nor did it require specialist training to understand. Which meant that the theologians, with their dialectical arguments, were merely confusing the issue. As for philosophy, it should be reserved for the elite few who had the intellectual capacity to undertake its study – think Plato and his philosopher-kings.

Having been translated into Hebrew and Latin, the works of Averroes continued to be studied in the West until the middle of the seventeenth century. In the Muslim world, however, his work was condemned by orthodox religious scholars, who rejected his opinion that religious law and philosophy shared the same goal.

◞◟

Maimonides

(1135–1204)

The Jewish philosopher and Talmudic scholar Maimonides, or Moses ben Maimon – he was also known as Rambam, from the first letters of his name: Rabbi Moshe ben Maimon – was born in Cordoba, where his father was a judge. When he was thirteen, the family left Spain. After several years on the move in North Africa, Maimonides eventually settled near Cairo in 1165, becoming leader of the Jewish community there. He studied Greek philosophy and medicine, and in 1183 was appointed physician to the vizier of the Sultan, Saladin – he of Crusader fame.

Maimonides was a prolific author whose best-known works are his *Guide to the Perplexed* – written originally in Arabic, although later Hebrew and Latin translations reached a much wider audience – and his authoritative fourteen-volume commentary on the

Mishnah, or code of Jewish law, the *Mishneh Torah*, which, understandably, was written in Hebrew. The 'perplexed' in question are students of Aristotelian philosophy confused by apparent contradictions between what they are studying and certain

---

APOPHATIC THEOLOGY

Bet you can't even say it! But when Maimonides was wrestling with those questions about the nature of God that so perplexed his students, this is what he came up with – and it's all to do with negating the attributes that might be applied to God.

Because God's existence is absolute, without composition, we cannot know his essence, only that he exists. Consequently it is wrong to assume that he has any positive attributes. Negative attributes are necessary to point our minds towards the truths we must believe. So when we say that something exists, what we mean is that its non-existence is impossible; it is living – it is not dead; it is the first – its existence has no cause; it has power, wisdom and will – it is not weak or ignorant; God is one – there is not more than one God. Every attribute put forward to convey some idea of God's nature denotes the negation of the opposite. Or so says the *Guide to the Perplexed* (1:58). Clear now?

---

statements in the Bible and the Talmud, especially about the nature of God. The aim of the *Guide* is to reconcile Aristotelian philosophy and the Greek sciences with the literal truth of the Old Testament: since all truth is one, the Bible, containing as it does the revealed word of God, can only be complementary to reason. So, to give an example, Maimonides explains that he rejects the Aristotelian view that matter is eternal on the basis of reason, not faith. If he had been convinced of the opposing view, he would have had no difficulty in interpreting the biblical creation narrative accordingly.

Despite the fact that he relied on reason, Maimonides believed beyond any shadow of doubt in the Bible as divine revelation. As he saw it, the task of the philosopher was to confirm rationally the truth of religion and to disprove doctrines that seemed to contradict divine revelation.

⊚⊚

Roger Bacon

(*c.* 1214–92)

WISE WORDS:

'There are two ways of acquiring knowledge, one through reason, the other by experiment.'

— *On Experimental Science*

Having studied at the universities of Oxford and Paris, Roger Bacon went on to gain a reputation for learning in a wide range of subjects, including philosophy, mathematics, science and alchemy. In 1256, he joined the Franciscan Order, the Catholic order founded by St Francis of Assisi. Not only did he make full use of the Greek and Arabic texts that had appeared in the West to pursue the recognized route of deductive reasoning, but he also developed the idea of using scientific experimentation to further understanding.

Around 1266, Pope Clement IV asked Bacon to draw up a programme of studies for use in the universities, including the most up-to-date ideas on philosophy, science and language, with a view to improving the Church's teaching of theology, and thus its authority. The first part of this undertaking, *Opus maius*, was quickly followed by *Opus minus* and *Opus tertium*.

Bacon distinguishes *experientia*, or experience, from *experimentum*, a set of scientific principles based on experience. Experience is innate, the knowledge of things that all animals have, while scientific principles based on experience have to be learned. And it is scientific principles that allow the discovery of new truths. He outlines experiments in mathematics, astronomy and optics, such as calculating the position of the heavenly bodies, proposals for reforming the calendar, identifying the colour spectrum produced by shining light through water, and writing hypothetically about spectacles and telescopes. He even describes flying machines and suggests that it might be possible to power ships and carriages mechanically.

When Pope Clement died in 1268, however, the Church authorities' enthusiasm for Bacon's educational methods died with him. Eventually, Bacon fell from favour with the Franciscans, too. By 1278, they had become suspicious of his experimental work, condemning him for what they referred to as 'suspected novelties' and possibly even imprisoning him for a while. And that was the end of Bacon's Church-and-science-working-together experiment.

UNI, MEDIEVAL-STYLE

The word 'university' is derived from the Latin *universitas magistrorum et scholarium*, meaning a community or corporation of masters and students. Before the formal establishment of universities as self-regulating centres of learning with academic freedom of expression, higher education was based in cathedral or monastic schools, where students were taught by monks and followed patterns of teaching laid down by the Church. Coinciding with the reintroduction of Aristotle's work to the West, the development of medieval universities saw the beginnings of a wider syllabus more familiar to modern students. Paris (1150) and Oxford (1167), where Roger Bacon and William of Ockham studied, are two of the oldest universities.

෧෧

Thomas Aquinas

(1225–74)

WISE WORDS:

'… for the knowledge of any truth whatsoever man needs Divine help.'

— Summa Theologica

Related to the Italian counts of Aquino, Thomas Aquinas was educated in the Benedictine monastery at Monte Cassino and at the University of Naples. Against the wishes of his family, who locked him up for a year to try to dissuade him, he then joined the Dominicans, a preaching order. He studied and taught in Cologne and Paris before being summoned to teach in Italy by Pope Alexander IV in 1258. Although once known as the Dumb Ox, presumably because of his build (he was a big chap) rather than his intellectual capabilities, he was publishing commentaries on Aristotle by his late twenties. Aquinas wanted to get back to Aristotle in the original, before earlier commentators such as Avicenna and Averroes had reformulated his ideas to fit their own theological frameworks. This was the start of a life spent refining a synthesis of Christian theology and Aristotelian reasoning that in many ways still underpins the doctrines of the Catholic Church.

Aquinas' take on the reason vs. faith argument was that they are separate but complementary, the first subservient without being subordinate. The world is full of real things that we can see and conceive of, but behind them there is a first cause. God's existence could be demonstrated through reason, while specific doctrines, such as the Trinity and the incarnation of Christ, were revealed through faith.

Aquinas was the author of two major texts, the *Summa contra Gentiles* (1259–64), a sort of handbook for Dominican missionaries, and the *Summa Theologica* (1266–73), which, though incomplete at the time of his death, laid out all the tenets of his Christian philosophy. The most famous of these is the *quinque viae* ('five ways'), which have become known as his five proofs for the existence of God. Using terminology from Aristotle's *Metaphysics*, Aquinas declares that God is the 'unmoved mover' who causes change in others (1 = change); the first cause that makes everything else happen (2 = dependence); the one non-contingent, necessary being supporting the existence of all other contingent things (3 = contingency); the greatest being from which lesser beings take whatever greatness they have (4 = limited perfection); the intelligent designer who directs non-intelligent things to act towards an end (5 = utility).

Aquinas evidently liked systems. As well as the five ways, he gives us five statements about the divine nature of God (he is simple, perfect, infinite, immutable and one), four cardinal virtues (prudence, temperance, justice and fortitude) and three theological virtues (faith, hope and charity).

ׁׁ

William of Ockham

(*c.* 1287–1347)

Born in Ockham, Surrey, William became a Franciscan friar before going on to study theology at Oxford. He never completed his degree or obtained a teaching post, presumably because his views rocked the boat – the chancellor of the university went so far as to accuse him of heresy. As a result, he was summoned to appear before Pope John XXII in Avignon, where he became embroiled in yet more controversy, this time about whether the Franciscans should stick to their vow of poverty. William said yes and the Pope said no – at which point, William decided it might be wise to make a hasty exit, although he was nonetheless excommunicated and spent the rest of his life under the protection of Emperor Louis IV of Bavaria.

In his best-known philosophical work, the *Summa Logicae*, William offers a new take on Aristotle and scholasticism, putting forward the view that there are no such things as over-arching universals, essences or forms. Instead, there are just individual objects and we are made aware of them by our minds, through a process referred to as intuitive cognition. When we need to think of several objects at once, we come up with terms such as 'universal', but these are only names, nothing more – which explains why William's doctrine is known as nominalism (from the Latin *nomen*, 'name'). Each individual object can have component parts, but it is always absolutely singular in itself. None of these individual objects is automatically the cause of another, nor the effect of another, while their coexistence does not alter the fact that they are singular. All of which led him to state, 'Plurality is never to be posited without need', which is a fancy way of saying 'Keep things simple' and is the principle behind Ockham's razor (see box).

William held that there was no way the existence of God could be demonstrated, whatever so-called 'proofs' other scholars advanced. But he saw no need to make the link between faith and reason. Faith for him was purely a matter of revelation.

OCKHAM'S (OR OCCAM'S) RAZOR

An expression that's heard more often than the name William of Ockham (or Occam in Latin). The idea is to use his razor to cut away unnecessary parts of an argument in order to get down to the essentials – more like a potato peeler, really … So if you're faced with conflicting arguments that seem equally valid, go for the one that relies on the fewest assumptions and can be pared down the most.

This is also known as the Law of Parsimony, although it might be better to replace 'parsimony' with 'pithy' here, because the idea can be boiled down to: the simplest solution is usually the best.

RENAISSANCE MEN

◎◎

Historians tend to go for 'Renaissance' – literally 'rebirth' – when they want a word to describe periods marked by a major revival of interest in ideas from antiquity. After the last chapter, it should come as no surprise to learn that there was a twelfth-century Renaissance: it's the term applied to the period of intellectual fervour that followed on from the rediscovery of Aristotle's works by Christian scholars. But the *real* Renaissance, the cultural one everyone knows about, started in fourteenth-century Italy, from where it spread into other parts of Europe over the course of the fifteenth and sixteenth centuries. Think Giotto, Brunelleschi, Donatello, Leonardo da Vinci and Michelangelo. It had an enormous impact on every area of intellectual life – not just art and architecture, but also literature, politics, science, religion and, of course, philosophy. Hence the expression 'Renaissance man' for someone who turns his hand to all manner of intellectual enquiry.

The classical texts that were of interest this time round were literary and historical. Turning away from medieval theology, intellectuals focused more closely on human concerns instead. They didn't reject Christianity – in fact, quite the reverse, as the Church remained an important patron throughout the period – but the way in which religion was approached began to shift. Realism and human sensibilities assumed much more importance, as in every field of study, which explains the name given to these intellectuals: Humanists. Through a revival of interest in the classical past, coupled with their new approach to learning, Renaissance Humanists attempted to deal with life on earth rather than focus on the afterlife. Which brings us to Erasmus and Machiavelli, two Renaissance men par excellence.

☯☯

Desiderius Erasmus

(1466–1536)

WISE WORDS:

'Among the blind the cross-eyed man is king.'

– Adages

Born in Rotterdam, Desiderius Erasmus was the son of a priest who had spent time in Italy studying Greek and Latin, and no doubt soaking up all that Renaissance spirit, before returning to his parish in the Netherlands. Erasmus was educated in Deventer, at one of the top Latin grammar schools in the country, and later in Hertogenbosch, at a school run by the Brethren of the Common Life – an association founded a century earlier to promote Christian values and worship. He was encouraged to join the Augustinian monastery at Steyn, near Gouda, which he did in 1487, and was ordained in 1492.

It must have been pretty obvious that Erasmus didn't want to stay in the monastery, however, because he immediately took a post with the Bishop of Cambrai, leaving him shortly afterwards to study theology and then teach in Paris. Here he came face to face for the first time with people who had been exposed to the full range of Humanist ideas spreading out from Italy. As a young man, he had questioned the constraints of traditional medieval scholasticism, but now in Paris he could give full rein to his wider interests. He embarked on a life of scholarship that would see him teaching across Europe, corresponding with leading thinkers of the day – such men as John Colet and Thomas More, for example – and publishing widely thanks to that wonderful new invention, the printing press.

Erasmus had no intention of breaking with the Catholic Church, but he wanted to apply critical reasoning to its teachings and practices. He spoke out against Church leaders' reliance on superstition and tradition to keep people in line, arguing instead for a return to a simpler, more rational piety based on a clear understanding of the Scriptures – he produced his own translation of the New Testament in Greek with this in mind. His best-known work, though, is *The Praise of Folly* – dedicated to Thomas More – in which he satirizes among other things some of the worst excesses of contemporary bishops, priests and monks: their worldliness, ignorance, greed and immorality just for starters.

Erasmus' criticisms reflected prevailing dissatisfaction with the Church, and were taken up by such reformers as Martin

Luther, but while Luther ultimately split the Church and ushered in the Protestant Reformation, Erasmus tried to keep out of the increasingly acrimonious religious disputes to which his writings contributed.

∾

Niccolò Machiavelli

(1469–1527)

WISE WORDS:

'It is much safer to be feared than loved when, of the two, either must be dispensed with.'

— *The Prince*

Someone who didn't advocate keeping out of disputes was the Florentine political philosopher Niccolò Machiavelli. Little is known about his early life, but in 1498 he was appointed to two administrative posts: secretary of the Second Chancery and secretary to the Council of Ten, which handled foreign affairs for the Florentine Republic. He took part in a number of diplomatic missions over the next fourteen years, in the course of which he met many of the most important political leaders of the time, including Louis XII of France, the Holy Roman Emperor Maximilian I, Pope Julius II and Cesare Borgia. His reports and letters make it clear that he studied these people and their actions with considerable enthusiasm and insight, and it was surely during this time that he developed the ideas that later appeared in his best-known work, *The Prince*.

The return in 1512 of the Medici, the previous rulers of Florence in practice if not in name, meant the end of both the republic and Machiavelli's diplomatic career. To make matters worse, the following year he was accused of conspiracy and tortured. Although he was pardoned, Machiavelli withdrew from public life and devoted himself to writing.

In the form of a letter to Lorenzo de' Medici, *The Prince* (1513, but not published until 1532) was intended as a handbook for rulers, with advice on what a prince should say and do to achieve and retain political power. Where, in the past, political theorists might have been concerned with how to promote the common good and act justly, Machiavelli was more interested in exploring the ways in which rulers could keep a tight grip on their position. And if murder was the most logical tack, so be it – getting rid of the previous ruling family was crucial.

The Prince advocates cruelty if it makes your subjects frightened of you and therefore malleable, but it should be swift and emphatic. Rewards, however, should be offered sparingly, to keep them wanting more. Deception must be practised because people are superficial, but rulers should always *pretend* to be virtuous, so as not to give their subjects any grounds for hatred.

In essence, *The Prince* is saying that rulers must be prepared to do bad things if they judge that the results will be worth it: the ends justify the means and so on. This shift from idealism to realism is Machiavelli's great contribution to political philosophy.

WAS MACHIAVELLI MACHIAVELLIAN?

Although he was also a historian, playwright and poet, Machiavelli is best known for *The Prince*, which explains why the word 'Machiavellian' is applied to someone who is cunning, scheming and unscrupulous, especially in the political sphere.

The Age of Reason

♋

All those certainties of the past – one Church, with the king ruling by divine right as God's representative on earth – had broken down big time by the seventeenth century. In England there was the Civil War between Royalists and Parliamentarians, culminating in the king losing his head, and throughout Europe there was ongoing conflict between Catholics and Protestants. The nature of the monarchy and the relationship between ruler and ruled were very much up for discussion. Fortunately, the fact that such thinkers as Hobbes and Locke (see pp.89 and 96) often had to take themselves off to other countries just to stay out of harm's way didn't prevent them from producing major works of political philosophy that are still in print today.

The detachment of philosophy from theology was well under way during this period. It's not that the existence of a deity was in doubt – despite Spinoza's expulsion from the Jewish community and accusations of atheism against, for example, Leibniz – but that blind faith was never going to be enough again. Arguments had to be put forward and supported, and in the seventeenth century there was an awful lot of interest in systems that might do the trick. For ease, we can distinguish two main approaches: rationalism and empiricism. In the rationalist camp were those who argued that reason – logical, mathematical, if-A-then-B reasoning – could provide the basis for all knowledge: Descartes, Spinoza and Leibniz (see pp.92, 98 and 102) were the main players. In the empiricist camp were those who believed that knowledge could come only through the senses, from experience: enter Hobbes and Locke, with their reliance on experiments in the natural sciences.

☯

Thomas Hobbes

(1588–1679)

WISE WORDS:

'The life of man [is] solitary, poor, nasty, brutish, and short.'

— *Leviathan*

Born in Malmesbury, Wiltshire – prematurely, when his poor mother heard that the Spanish Armada was on its way, or so he liked to tell people – Thomas Hobbes was educated at Oxford and then worked as a tutor, mainly to members of the Cavendish family, the Earls of Devonshire. In this capacity he travelled widely, meeting many of the leading intellectual figures of the day, including Galileo and Descartes (see p.92).

At the age of forty, Hobbes became fascinated by Euclidean geometry and the idea that its certainties might be applicable to a study of people and society – in other words, that there might be similar rules governing political science. As this was a time of increasing unrest in England, with the Civil War looming, his preoccupations were hardly surprising. And when, just as Parliament was flexing its democratic muscles against Charles I, Hobbes reached the conclusion, in his *Elements of Law Natural and Political*, that monarchy was the best form of government, he decided that exile was the wisest course and fled to France. He remained for eleven years, until 1651, and even tutored the future Charles II while there.

In 1642, Hobbes completed *De Cive* ('About the Citizen'), in which he first put forward his ideas on the origins of civil society. It was not translated into English until 1651, by which time he had fleshed out these ideas into his major work, *Leviathan: The Matter, Forme, and Power of a Commonwealth Ecclesiasticall and Civil* (1651), with reflections on metaphysics, psychology and political philosophy.

After his visit to Galileo in 1636, Hobbes had incorporated the science of mechanics and motion into his thinking as a way to explain human behaviour. A materialist, he believed the world to be a purely mechanical system made up of nothing but matter in motion, driven by forces of attraction and repulsion under the laws of nature. These forces governed human behaviour and determined what people considered 'good' (attractive) and 'bad' (repulsive). Because humans are wholly selfish in the state of nature, they fight each other for what they need, which can lead only to war and the nasty shortness of life noted in the quotation at the start of this entry. To avoid this, in a spirit of enlightened self-interest, humans agree to a social contract whereby each surrenders a bit of independence for the greater good. The resulting civil society exists under a sovereign with absolute power, to whom everyone agrees to defer in return for protection from war. Only if he fails to deliver on the protection front should the sovereign expect trouble. Otherwise, in order to be effective, he has every right to total control of civil, military, judicial and ecclesiastical matters.

Hobbes must have known his views would offend all sorts of people. His support for the monarchy upset Parliamentarians, but by denying the divine right of kings he upset many Royalists (although interestingly not Charles II himself, who always had a soft spot for his old tutor). As for the Church, accusations of atheism led some clergymen to recommend burning not only his books but Hobbes himself – once again, Charles II stepped in to put a stop to that one.

WHAT A BEAST

Leviathan is the name of the beast from the depths, the great sea monster referred to in the Book of Job (41:34): '… he *is* a king over all the children of pride'. Hobbes himself was dubbed 'the Beast of Malmesbury' by opponents.

NEVER MIND HARRY POTTER …

Towards the end of his life, Hobbes invited friends to come up with suggestions for his epitaph. Apparently, the one he thought would look best carved on his gravestone read 'This is the true philosopher's stone', but for some reason it was not used.

◎◎

René Descartes

(1596–1650)

WISE WORDS:

'I think, therefore I am.'

— *Discourse on Method*

The philosopher whose words gave this book its title was born in France at La Haye en Touraine, which was subsequently renamed La Haye Descartes in his honour. Educated at the Jesuit college of La Flèche in Anjou, he would have had a thorough grounding in the scholasticism he was later to question. Descartes then studied law at Poitiers, but rather than practising, he opted to reflect on life for a while, so he went to the Dutch Republic in 1618 and enlisted in the army of Maurice of Nassau. The following year, while serving in Germany, he had a series of visions that showed him how the whole of philosophy – and knowledge in general, come to that – could be recast as a unified system of truths based on mathematics and supported by rationalism. In 1628, after ten more years reflecting his way round Europe, Descartes settled in Holland, where he spent most of the rest of his life. It was here that he wrote his major works, *Discourse on Method* (1637), *Meditations on First Philosophy* (1641) and *Principles of Philosophy* (1644).

The starting point for Descartes is the quest for certainties – never an easy matter, he realizes, as the senses can be deceived. The method he proposes to use is known as hyperbolic doubt – 'hyperbolic' in the sense of 'extreme'. So to test how grounded in reason our so-called 'knowledge' is, we need to suspend judgement on any proposition whose truth can in any way be doubted. By a process of elimination, Descartes arrives at his famous conclusion, *Cogito, ergo sum* ('I think, therefore I am'). He is certain of his own existence, otherwise he would not be thinking.

Descartes then takes a look at *what* he is thinking, identifying among other things the idea of a Perfect Being, or God. He is sure that this is true and must exist outside his mind, because otherwise the *cogito* itself would not be true. Which sounds like scholasticism again, although this time, the Perfect Being helps prove the reliability of human reasoning: he is God 'in whom all the wisdom of the sciences lies hid'. Since God leads Descartes to believe that things in the external world are material, they must be, because a perfect God would not deceive him. And just as in the wax test (see box), it is reason rather than perception that tells Descartes he can trust the evidence of his senses. This dualism – Cartesian dualism, no less: the split between the non-material, thinking mind and the material, mechanistic body – is something that continues to interest people to this day.

Descartes was not without his critics right from the start, but when Queen Christina of Sweden decided in 1649 that she wanted philosophy lessons, he was the one she summoned. Unfortunately for Descartes, the venture was not a success. To begin with, Christina liked to start at five in the morning, even though it was the middle of winter and he was the sort of man who preferred a quiet morning in bed, reading and doing a bit more reflecting. He died of pneumonia within six months of arriving.

CARTESIAN COORDINATES

In his spare time, Descartes was a mathematician of note and anyone who's ever wrestled with graph paper in a maths lesson, plotting x and y coordinates, has René to blame. His system allows you to locate points on a plane by means of paired coordinates, which also means you can express geometric shapes as algebraic equations … should you wish to. It might not be much fun in class, but it comes in very handy when map-reading.

TAKE THE WAX TEST

Hold a piece of wax to a candle flame and it will change texture, shape and size. Is it still wax? Yes, even though it looks and feels quite different. 'And so,' Descartes says, 'something which I thought I was seeing with my eyes is in fact grasped solely by the faculty of judgment which is in my mind' (*Meditations on First Philosophy*).

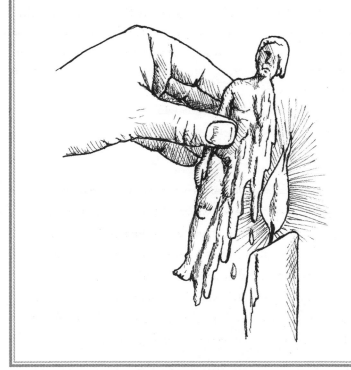

๑๑

John Locke

(1632–1704)

WISE WORDS:

'… we can have knowledge no further than we have ideas.'

— *An Essay Concerning Human Understanding*

Born in Somerset, John Locke was educated at Oxford, where he found himself completely out of step with what he considered the obsolete scholastic philosophy of the time. Instead he was much more interested in the experiments in physics and chemistry being carried out in Oxford at the time by people such as Robert Boyle – he of Boyle's Law, the one about the relationship between the pressure and volume of a gas – and the study of medicine. In 1667, he joined the household of prominent politician Lord Ashley as a doctor and adviser in scientific and political affairs, coming into contact with leading figures in London as a result. When Ashley became the first Earl of Shaftesbury and Charles II's Lord Chancellor in 1672, Locke was given a government position, but he retired and took himself off to France in 1675, ostensibly for reasons of health but possibly on political grounds, too. In 1683, he went to Holland, where he became involved with English supporters of William of Orange, and did not return to England until after the Glorious Revolution of 1688, which saw William of Orange and his wife, Mary, crowned William III and Mary II.

In his *Two Treatises of Government* (1690), Locke sets out his political philosophy, which provides justification for the revolution. He disputes the traditional idea that kings have a divine right to rule as God's representatives on earth, and takes the social contract a step further than did Hobbes, by incorporating the sovereign. In a state of nature, before anyone has even thought about coming together to form a government, people have the right to defend their life, their health and their property. In order to settle disputes about such matters, they agree to form a government that will protect their rights. But that government rules *only* with the consent of the governed; should it fail to look after their rights, it loses its legitimacy and can justifiably be overthrown – which explains why these ideas were so popular in eighteenth-century America, which sought independence from Britain, and in France, which sought the heads of its monarchs.

Locke's major philosophical work, *An Essay Concerning Human Understanding* (1690), was some twenty years in the making, which isn't so surprising once you know that he wanted 'to inquire into the origin, certainty and extent of human knowledge' – no mean task. Our minds, he says, are like blank canvases to begin with; we have no innate ideas. But once we start to sense things, the first simple ideas come, and from these 'ideas of sensation' we move on a stage further to 'ideas of reflection' – knowledge that results from reflecting on our sensory experiences. So consciousness, perception and thought all spring ultimately from experience. Which makes Locke an empiricist: someone who believes that knowledge is based on experience derived from the senses. And this harks right back to his early belief in the value of scientific experimentation.

CREDIT CRUNCH

Locke wasn't just a philosopher. His snappily titled *Some Considerations on the Consequences of the Lowering of Interest and the Raising of the Value of Money* (1691) could teach the bankers of today a thing or two.

⊚⊘

Baruch Spinoza
(1632–77)

WISE WORDS:

'A free man is one who lives under the guidance of reason, who is not led by fear, but who directly desires that which is good.'

— *Ethics*

The Dutch philosopher also known as Benedictus de Spinoza (Baruch and Benedictus both mean 'blessed', in Hebrew and Latin respectively) was born in Amsterdam into a Jewish family that had fled Portugal to escape Catholic persecution. Religion obviously remained problematic, because in 1656 he was expelled from the Jewish community, his freethinking approach too much for the synagogue authorities.

By trade, Spinoza was a lens grinder and polisher, and that's how he made his living, but he devoted his life to the study of ideas, corresponding over many years with other scientific and philosophical writers. As his fame spread, a society was formed to discuss his works, and from 1663 his home near The Hague was a meeting place for leading intellectuals of the day. That same year, he published *The Principles of Descartes' Philosophy*, the only work to appear under his name during his lifetime. In 1673, he turned down the chance to teach philosophy at Heidelberg University because he wanted the freedom to continue his own research, but he died of consumption four years later, possibly because of all the glass powder he'd inhaled.

Spinoza's views on religion first appeared in print in his *Theologico-Political Treatise*, which was published anonymously in 1670 and banned in 1674, having offended the religious authorities. Here he suggests that the Bible should be interpreted by careful study alone, rather than with a view to supporting preconceived ideas or doctrines, and acknowledges that this might reveal many beliefs about God and the universe to be false. What's more, he says that God acts only according to the laws of his own nature, not with any particular purpose in mind. It all added up to an argument for religious tolerance, so was understandably unpopular in certain quarters.

Even more controversial was the *Ethics* (1677), which could not be published until after Spinoza's death. Each of its five parts is treated like a mathematical problem, opening with a set of definitions and axioms from which Spinoza deduces

THE INVISIBLE COLLEGE

It sounds like Harry Potter again, but this was the name given by Robert Boyle to the group of natural scientists who met regularly to exchange ideas and discuss their experiments. The College was the precursor to the Royal Society, which was founded in London in 1660. Henry Oldenburg, the Royal Society's first secretary, corresponded with Spinoza for some fifteen years, while Leibniz went there to demonstrate the calculating machine he had designed and built. A large metal contraption operated by cranks and dials, Leibniz's Stepped Reckoner was the first machine of its kind to not only add and subtract, but also multiply and divide.

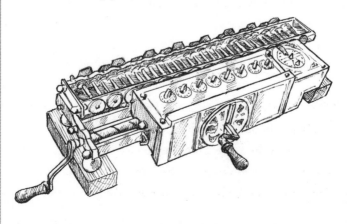

theorems, or proofs. Rejecting Descartes' mind–body dualism, he concludes that there is only one substance, which is both God and nature. This amounts to pantheism: the belief that God can be identified with nature and nature is a manifestation of God. For Spinoza, nature is both infinite and perfect. Everything, including human beings, is an aspect of nature, which operates – again – according to its own necessity. This means there's no such thing as chance or free will; anyone who thinks they have free will just doesn't understand the causes determining their actions. Nor is there any objective good or evil – such things depend on your standpoint. Happiness will never be achieved by acquiring possessions or through the emotions. A life of reason is the only way forward, and the greatest good comes from knowledge of God.

For Spinoza, then, the fundamental philosophical questions are to be answered not by experiment but through the use of reason – which makes him a rationalist.

CHOCO LEIBNIZ

There's a connection – there really is – between the great philosopher and the equally great chocolate biscuits. When the Hanover-based manufacturers Bahlsen were looking for the name of a famous resident to use on the box, Leibniz was their first choice.

༙༙

Gottfried Wilhelm Leibniz

(1646–1716)

WISE WORDS:

'Nothing happens without a sufficient reason, why it should be so, rather than otherwise.'

– Letter to Samuel Clarke, *A Collection of Papers,*
Which passed between the late Learned Mr. Leibnitz, and
Dr. Clarke, In the Years 1715 and 1716

Born in Leipzig, where his father was Professor of Moral Philosophy at the university, Gottfried Wilhelm Leibniz started his studies there at the age of fourteen. He graduated in 1663 and then studied jurisprudence for three years, publishing a paper on legal education that impressed the Elector of Mainz, for whom he went to work.

The Elector was keen to explore ways of keeping the peace in Europe – these were troubled times, with France looking aggressively in Germany's direction – and Leibniz set to work defining a rational foundation for Christianity that would suit both Catholics and Protestants, thus encouraging religious tolerance. Having gone on a diplomatic mission to Louis XIV, Leibniz stayed in France for four years, mixing with leading intellectuals, and also visited London, where he was elected a member of the Royal Society. In 1676, when the Elector of Mainz died, Leibniz became Librarian to the Duke of Brunswick at Hanover. On his way back to Hanover, he visited Spinoza (see p.98), who had just completed the *Ethics*. For the rest of his life, Leibniz carried out his court duties while compiling a history of the House of Brunswick and developing his own work, which now exists mainly in the form of unpublished papers and letters.

In *Theodicy* (1710), one of his few books, Leibniz discusses how to reconcile the existence of an all-powerful, benevolent God with the fact of general unpleasantness in the world. He invokes the sufficient-reason principle, which holds that everything has a reason to exist, and to exist in just the way it does. So in the case of God deciding what sort of world to create, he must have had sufficient reason for creating the one we're living in. And because God is morally perfect, his choice must have been determined by the value of our world. Which in turn means that our world must be the best possible. It was this 'best possible world' thing that Voltaire (see p.109) pilloried so mercilessly in his novel *Candide*, as one disaster after another befell the protagonists.

The late work *Monadology* (1714) contains Leibniz's conclusions about the composition of the universe. It is made up, he says, of ultimate substances called monads (from the Greek *monos*, 'alone'), each of which is eternal and incorruptible. Despite appearances to the contrary, these monads do not interact with each other causally – cause and effect are illusions, as are space and time. Rather, each monad is busy following pre-programmed instructions and behaves as it does purely because that is part of its identity: a monad is 'pregnant' with the future and 'laden' with the past, just like a seed. The benevolent God has willed their pre-established harmony, each one of them a tiny reflection of the universe.

Leibniz wrote widely on a range of subjects – history, law and political theory, for starters – and made major contributions to the study of mathematics. He and Isaac Newton both claimed to have developed calculus; then there was his calculating machine (see p.100), not to mention work on statistics and probability theory. He saw the logic inherent in mathematics as the way to refine philosophical reasoning and check objectively for mistakes in arguments – the perfect way to settle disputes rationally.

THE AGE OF ENLIGHTENMENT

A massive outpouring of intellectual, scientific and cultural activity in the eighteenth century both fostered and was fed by a range of philosophical ideas, all of which competed with each other in applying the analytical methods Isaac Newton had used so successfully in the natural world to the study of mankind. The sense that the dark clouds of ignorance could be dispelled by a rigorous questioning of traditional values explains why the period is known as the Age of Enlightenment. From now on, reason was to be the only yardstick, and who better to come up with a systematic approach than philosophers?

Unsurprisingly, different philosophers reached different conclusions based on their own definitions of reason, so enlightenment took many forms, and it is clear that ideas of great moment were being discussed. Freedom and democracy were up for discussion, plus further questioning of religious beliefs and authority. Taken together with ideas about the contractual basis of rights, they would lead to all sorts of political upheavals: the American and French revolutions, to name just a couple.

There was no going back. As Kant said in an essay entitled 'Answering the Question: What is Enlightenment?' (1784), 'Enlightenment is man's emergence from his self-incurred immaturity.' His rallying cry was: 'Dare to know!'

∞∞

George Berkeley
(1685–1753)

WISE WORDS:

'... *esse* is *percipi* [to be is to be perceived].'
— *A Treatise Concerning the Principles
of Human Knowledge*

Born near Kilkenny, George Berkeley was educated at Trinity College Dublin, becoming a fellow there in 1707. He was ordained a deacon in 1709 and a priest the following year.

Berkeley's most important philosophical works were published relatively early in his life: *Essay towards a New Theory of Vision* in 1709, *A Treatise Concerning the Principles of Human Knowledge* in 1710 and *Three Dialogues between Hylas and Philonous* in 1713. He visited London in 1713, then spent several years travelling in Italy and France. When he returned to Ireland in 1721, he was plainly worried about the decadence and corruption he had witnessed during his time away, as he wrote the anonymous *Essay towards Preventing the Ruin of Great Britain*, 'an attack on luxury both as an economic and as a political and moral evil'. Around the same time, he became wildly enthusiastic about the idea of establishing a university in Bermuda, with a view to spreading the gospel 'among the American savages' – no doubt to prevent ruin there, too. He was made Dean of Derry in 1724 and, after lobbying in London to get support for his project, he and his new wife sailed west in 1728. They settled temporarily in Rhode Island to await the promised funds, but these never materialized. After three years, he abandoned his dream, returning home, and in 1734 he was made Bishop of Cloyne.

Berkeley was not only an empiricist but also a leading idealist, a word that in the philosophical sense has nothing to do with pursuing worthy aims but refers to the theory that physical objects don't exist outside the mind that perceives them; which makes them ideas, hence idealism. Berkeley saw himself as a man of common sense and he was obviously religious. He was deeply troubled, therefore, by the scope for scepticism – as in denying the possibility of knowledge – and atheism that he identified in the approach taken by John Locke (see p.96), with its emphasis on materialism: scepticism because the senses can mislead about the nature of material things, which might not even exist in the first place; atheism because it's possible for a material world to work without divine involvement.

The way forward came to Berkeley like a revelation: he denied the existence of matter. So, taking the example of an apple, 'a certain colour, taste, smell, figure and consistence having been observed to go together, are accounted one distinct thing, signified by the name apple' – that's all an apple is. And does it still exist if no one perceives it? Well, Berkeley's answer was that, thanks to the existence of an omnipresent God, the apple was always being perceived. And what causes ideas in the first place? That's God again, because only God, being omniscient, could manage such an undertaking. As to what becomes of scientific theories if matter is denied, the answer is straightforward enough: they apply to the world of our experience, enabling us to predict outcomes, and that's all – they don't exist beyond our minds.

On a less spiritual level, one of Berkeley's most popular works – a bestseller in his lifetime – was *Siris* (1744), in which with evangelical zeal he spread the word about the medicinal benefits of tar water, a miracle cure for all ailments.

UNIVERSITY OF CALIFORNIA, BERKELEY

One of the best universities in the world today was formed when the College of California and the Agricultural, Mining, and Mechanical Arts College merged in 1868 to create the University of California. And who did the authorities decide to name their university after? The good bishop, of course, thanks to his enlightened ideas about colonial education ... So Berkeley got his university after all.

◎◎

Voltaire

(1694–1778)

WISE WORDS:

'Doubt is not a pleasant condition. But certainty is an absurd one.'

— Letter to Frederick the Great, 28 November 1770

François-Marie Arouet was born in Paris and educated by Jesuits at the Collège Louis-le-Grand. From his early twenties, his satirical writings got him into trouble, leading to periods of banishment from Paris and even imprisonment in the Bastille. It was during one stay inside that he adopted the name Voltaire. In 1726, he was let out of prison on the condition that he left for England immediately, and he spent the next three years there, mixing with leading literary and political figures of the day. He was very much taken with the concepts of civil liberties and constitutional monarchy he encountered, and also with the empirical approach taken by John Locke (see p.96) and Isaac Newton, who were to provide him with a rational framework to challenge what he saw as superstition and ignorance in his own country.

Voltaire had already produced poems, plays and essays, but from this time on, his writing took a more overtly philosophical turn. Back in France, he started work on his *Philosophical Letters on the English Nation* (1734), which conveyed his admiration for the liberal attitudes he'd come across in England. These stood in marked contrast to the norms in France, with its absolute monarch, entrenched aristocracy and pronounced religious intolerance, and Voltaire now devoted himself to challenging the power of the establishment. His book was the cue for more threats against him, and this time he retreated to the country to avoid arrest. In 1750, he left France for the Prussian court at the request of Frederick the Great, and although the two fell out after a few years, their correspondence continued.

Voltaire made his next home in Switzerland, settling near Geneva in 1755, and it was while living there that he published *Candide* (1759). The novel satirizes the philosophy of Leibniz (p.102) through the mouth of Dr Pangloss, Candide's tutor, who assures his charge that absolutely everything – earthquake, war, rape, murder, you name it – happens for the best 'in this best of all possible worlds' (see box for more pearls of wisdom). Voltaire was a deist – a believer in the existence of a supreme being – rather than a Christian, having seen too much of the damage organized religion could cause. His *Philosophical Dictionary* (1764), a pocket-sized book for people to carry round with them, contained entries that argued once more against the Church for its encouragement of superstition, repression and intolerance, and advocated freedom of expression.

A prolific writer (there were historical and scientific works, plus a vast correspondence as well), a constant thorn in the side of Church and State, and a champion of reason, Voltaire embodied the Enlightenment, while his ideas were to influence the French Revolution, which was only just round the corner.

THE WORLD ACCORDING TO PANGLOSS

As Dr Pangloss, learned Professor of Metaphysico-theologico-cosmolo-nigology, tells Candide, 'things cannot be otherwise than as they are; for all being created for an end, all is necessarily for the best end. Observe, that the nose has been formed to bear spectacles – thus we have spectacles. Legs are visibly designed for stockings – and we have stockings.' Even the fact that he has contracted syphilis doesn't diminish his optimism, 'for if Columbus had not in an island of America caught this disease, which contaminates the source of life, frequently even hinders generation, and which is evidently opposed to the great end of nature, we should have neither chocolate nor cochineal'. So that's all right, then.

෧෧

David Hume

(1711–76)

WISE WORDS:

'The great advantage of the mathematical sciences above
the moral consists in this, that the ideas of the former,
being sensible, are always clear and determinate.'

— An Enquiry Concerning Human Understanding

Born in Edinburgh, David Hume studied at the university there,
took up and abandoned a career in law, worked as a clerk in
Bristol and then, in 1734, went off to La Flèche in France, where
Descartes (see p.92) had been educated. He stayed three years,
studying and working on his first and most important book, *A
Treatise of Human Nature* (1739–40), before returning eventually to Scotland. The book's subtitle, *An Attempt to Introduce the
Experimental Method of Reasoning into Moral Subjects*, makes it
clear that Hume intended to take to its logical conclusion the
work of earlier empiricists such as Locke and Berkeley (see pp.96
and 106), rooting out any explanations that depended on 'invention [rather] than experience'. He divided his *Treatise* into three
sections – 'Of the Understanding', 'Of the Passions' and 'Of
Morals' – which between them encompassed his ideas on perception, causation, identity and ethics as they related to individuals
and society. However, despite its sweeping ambition, the book
fell on deaf ears when it first appeared.

'... NOTHING BUT SOPHISTRY
AND ILLUSION'

Reasoning, said Hume, is about discovering rela-
tionships between things. He identified two different
sorts: 'relations of ideas' and 'matters of fact'. That
15 is half of 30, for example, can be discovered and
demonstrated by reason alone, without reference to
other forms of evidence, so belongs in the first category. Statements such as 'The sun will rise
tomorrow', however, cannot be demonstrated by
reason alone; as long as their negation is conceiv-
able, we depend on experience to determine whether
they are true or false – which means they belong in
the second category.

For Hume, mathematics was the only worthwhile
form of demonstrative reasoning. Books that did not
contain mathematical demonstrations or empirical
reasoning – he singled out those on metaphysics and
theology in particular – deserved to be 'committed to
the flames' as nothing but ...

Undeterred, Hume went on to produce *Essays Moral and
Political* (1741–2), which had an immediate impact, and his
literary reputation began to grow. A reworking of the *Treatise*,

now entitled *An Enquiry Concerning Human Understanding* (1748) and *An Enquiry Concerning the Principles of Morals* (1751), followed. He also published a six-volume *History of England* (1754–62).

Recognized as a leading man of letters, in 1763 Hume was appointed secretary to the British ambassador in Paris, where he mixed with the French literary elite. In 1766, he accompanied leading Enlightenment figure Jean-Jacques Rousseau (see p.115) to England, but the trip ended disastrously with a major falling-out. Accused of being an atheist in his lifetime, Hume delayed publication of his last philosophical work, *Dialogues Concerning Natural Religion*; it was not published until 1779.

Hume's main arguments appear in the *Treatise*. The mind, he says, consists of perceptions, of which there are two kinds: impressions (sensations, passions and emotions), which are forceful and lively; and ideas (thinking and reasoning), which are faint copies of them. We cannot say that these impressions represent real objects because we have no real objects to compare them with. We might *think* we live in a world of objects that exist in time and space, ordered by causal laws, but that's just the result of custom and habit, with past experience determining what we expect to see. As for the passions, they are what make us act, preceding reason every time. What's more, ethical or moral certainties cannot be deduced from descriptions of things as, say, 'good' or 'bad'; these are just personal assessments. It is only because such scepticism is not a helpful way to live that, for practical purposes, we agree that our senses are telling us about real things.

Rather than going on from this position to suggest some

form of ultimate reality, Hume put forward a naturalist, non-metaphysical account – no supreme being, no first principles – based solely on experience and observation. Although he was more famous in his lifetime as a historian, his attempts to clarify how we know what we know have had a major influence on subsequent philosophers.

☯

Jean-Jacques Rousseau
(1712–78)

WISE WORDS:

'Man is born free; and everywhere he is in chains.'

— The Social Contract

Born in the Calvinist (strictly Protestant) city of Geneva, Jean-Jacques Rousseau had an unsettled childhood. His mother died just a few days after his birth, and ten years later his father fled to avoid imprisonment, leaving Rousseau to be brought up by an uncle. He had little formal education and left Geneva in 1728, wandering round Italy and Savoy before finally moving to Paris in 1742.

Here Rousseau made his living as a secretary and music copyist. After writing his own opera, he came to the attention of Voltaire (see p.109) and then Denis Diderot (see box overleaf), as a result of which he contributed entries to the *Encyclopédie* on music (1749) and then political economy (1755). In a prize-winning essay of 1750, *Discourse on the Arts and Sciences*, Rousseau had argued that advancements in these areas, rather than being beneficial, corrupted people's natural goodness and limited their freedom, while in *Discourse on the Origin and Basis of Inequality Among Men* (1754) he developed his theme that people are essentially good, not to mention free, when in a state of nature, but are corrupted and made unhappy by their experiences in society – society being an artificial construct that can be traced back to the first person fencing off a bit of land and effectively shouting, 'Mine!' These ideas were to reappear in his most important work of political philosophy, *The Social Contract* (1762).

In it, Rousseau argues for an arrangement – the contract of his book's title – whereby, in return for the protection given by society, individuals surrender their natural rights to the collective 'general will'. Sovereignty, which for Rousseau means the power to make laws, resides in this general will of the people and so can only represent the common good. The resulting laws are then enacted by the government. Liberty and equality will automatically follow for all, as the general will protects one person against the will of another, while laws that have been made collectively cannot impinge on individual freedoms (though it is made clear that anyone who disagrees will 'be forced to be free' – in their own best interests, of course). Rousseau did concede that the kind of republican government he was advocating would work best in a small city-state – somewhere like Geneva, for example – rather than a large country, but the idea of the state having a collective, overriding will of its own is one that's been accepted by many a large country since.

Rousseau's ideas about education were also to be very influential. In his book *Emile* (1762), he recommends that children's natural tendencies should be encouraged to develop rather than curbed or disciplined, and that learning should come from example rather than from books or lectures. Which is quite odd once you know that Rousseau abandoned his five children to foundling hospitals.

ENCYCLOPÉDIE

When, in 1745, the Parisian publisher and printer André le Breton decided to have Ephraim Chambers' *Cyclopaedia* (1728) translated from English into French, he could have had no idea what he was embarking on. After several false starts, Denis Diderot became chief editor of the *Encyclopédie ou Dictionnaire Raisonné des Sciences, des Arts et des Métiers*, with Jean le Rond d'Alembert as his editor. Between 1751 and 1765, seventeen volumes were published, with entries on every branch of knowledge, including philosophy, mathematics, politics and religion. Many of the best-known figures of the French Enlightenment contributed, including Voltaire and Rousseau (see pp.109 and 115).

◎◎

Immanuel Kant

(1724–1804)

WISE WORDS:

'Act only on that maxim whereby thou canst at the same time will that it should become a universal law.'

— *Groundwork of the Metaphysic of Morals*

The son of a saddler, Immanuel Kant was born in Königsberg, East Prussia, and lived there or nearby his whole life. He studied at the university, where he then taught as a lecturer, before becoming Professor of Logic and Metaphysics in 1770. Renowned for his quiet and orderly way of life (see box), Kant made much more of an impression with his philosophical works.

In *The Critique of Pure Reason* (1781), he produces a synthesis of the rationalism of Leibniz (see p.102), which holds that all knowledge is derived from deductions based on existing ideas, and the empiricism of Hume (see p.112), which holds that all knowledge is derived from observation alone. He concludes that we rely on the structure of our mind for our knowledge of the world, pure reason being something that can be known prior (*a priori*) to experience. In other words, the mind is no blank canvas passively waiting for objects to impinge upon it; instead, it plays an active part in acquiring knowledge by processing the information it perceives. And what we perceive in objects is the

WHAT'S THE TIME, MR KANT?

According to Heinrich Heine, in his book *On the History of Religion and Philosophy in Germany* (1832), 'I do not believe that the great clock of the cathedral [in Königsberg] performed in a more passionless and methodical manner its daily routine than did its townsman, Immanuel Kant. Rising in the morning, coffee-drinking, writing, reading lectures, dining, walking, everything had its appointed time, and the neighbours knew that it was exactly half-past three when Immanuel Kant stepped forth from his house in his grey, tight-fitting coat, with his Spanish cane in hand, and betook himself to the little linden avenue called to this day "Philosopher's Walk".'

result of our make-up as an observer rather than anything to do with the objects themselves.

Kant felt his conclusions were the equivalent in philosophy of a Copernican revolution – referring to the ground-breaking discovery made by the astronomer Nicolas Copernicus that the sun was the centre of the universe. He identifies categories such as time and space, which don't exist externally and therefore can't be learned from experience; instead, they are the basic concepts of the framework that helps us make sense of the world. Effectively, though the mind does not *create* the world, it does constitute the way the world appears.

For Kant, both the nature of reality and human morality are grounded in reason, which is the underlying principle of moral philosophy. Just as there is a law of nature, so there is a moral law, each of them the result of our mind imposing order on the welter of information received. In the *Groundwork of the Metaphysic of Morals* (1785), Kant refines his supreme moral law, the famous categorical imperative (see the quotation that starts this entry). Basically, if you want to do the right thing, adopt behaviour that you would happily see applied as a universal principle, and which allows you to treat other people as ends in themselves, not merely as means to your ends.

The Critique of Practical Reason (1788) also deals with ethics and the search for moral laws, while *The Critique of Judgement* (1790) covers aesthetic judgements, leading on to theology, too: from art, via artist conveying the beauties of nature, to the creator of that beautiful nature. As with his views on perception and ethics, Kant was seeking to establish an *a priori* principle of aesthetics to explain our apprehension of beauty.

Kant's philosophy, which he himself described as 'transcendental' or 'critical' idealism, attempted to reconcile the authority of science – taking into account the revolution in the natural sciences brought about by men such as Copernicus – with people's everyday experience of a world bursting with moral, aesthetic, cultural and religious concerns.

CONFUSED YET?

If not, try this from Kant's *Critique of Pure Reason*: 'The assertorical speaks of logical reality or truth; as, for example, in a hypothetical syllogism, the antecedens presents itself in a problematical form in the major, in an assertorical form in the minor, and it shows that the proposition is in harmony with the laws of the understanding. The apodeictical proposition cogitates the assertorical as determined by these very laws of the understanding, consequently as affirming *a priori*, and in this manner it expresses logical necessity.' Well, that's that sorted, then ...

INTO THE NINETEENTH CENTURY

The French Revolution and its after-effects left Europe a legacy of political turmoil in the late eighteenth and early nineteenth centuries. The democratic ideals, the descent into bloodthirsty chaos and the Napoleonic Wars set in train revolutionary rumblings at a time when advances in science and technology were empowering social groups not normally known for their political clout. Popular revolutions broke out in 1848 – the date of Marx's *Communist Manifesto* – in France and Germany. While the workers of the world were being exhorted to unite, fired up by socialist, communist and anarchist ideas, their capitalist masters were espousing free-market liberalism. In the 1870s, maps had to be redrawn as nationalist movements in Germany and Italy saw the unification of those countries into the entities we recognize today. And behind all the political, social and economic upheavals, the philosophers were at work – sometimes producing theories that explained what they were witnessing, but occasionally seeming to create the impetus for action.

〲〱

Jeremy Bentham

(1748–1832)

WISE WORDS:

'… the greatest happiness of the greatest number is
the foundation of morals and legislation.'

— *The Commonplace Book*

The son and grandson of lawyers, Jeremy Bentham was destined
for a legal career. Born in London, he went to Oxford at the
age of twelve and was admitted to Lincoln's Inn when only
fifteen. However, he soon decided that the law was too bound
up in irrational technicalities – he was particularly critical of
England's foremost legal theorist, Sir William Blackstone – and
so made it his mission to clarify the foundations of a just and
rational legal system.

The basis for Bentham's ideas, as laid out in his *Introduction
to the Principles of Morals and Legislation* (1789), is utility: 'that
property in any object, whereby it tends to produce benefit,
advantage, pleasure, good, or happiness … or … to prevent the
happening of mischief, pain, evil, or unhappiness'.

The way to judge if an action is right is by measuring its
tendency to promote the greatest happiness for the greatest
number, a philosophy known as utilitarianism. Happiness
equals pleasure (including the absence of pain) and is achieved
through the use of law and reason – the right law will produce

happiness, the right law being the one that accords with reason, and thus with the principle of utility. To work out how likely an action is to promote happiness, Bentham devised a felicific or hedonistic ('happiness-inducing') calculus that took into account such things as the intensity, duration and likelihood of pleasures and pains.

Keen on putting his ideas into practice, Bentham designed his famous prison, the Panopticon. This was a circular structure in which the prisoners were incarcerated around a central observation tower, unable to tell whether they were being watched at any given moment – or indeed whether there was anyone in the tower at all – thereby being trained to monitor

their own behaviour. Bentham believed that, since all punishment is pain, it is only justified if it is outweighed by the reduction in pain (or increase in pleasure) it causes in somebody else. So it's OK if people are deterred from doing things that would lead to more pain, but there's no point in punishment for punishment's sake.

For Bentham, there weren't any such things as natural rights or duties, or social contracts, either. The only rights were those based on law, linked with an authority to impose them on grounds of utility. Once people start talking about moral rights they are appealing to a higher moral authority – which is irrational. Anyway, apart from these theoretical objections, he blamed appeals to natural rights for the horrific violence of the French Revolution.

Bentham had hoped that politicians would see the advantage of introducing reforms to promote public happiness, but when they didn't, his enthusiasm for democratic reforms and wider voting rights grew. He thought that, with educational improvements, more and more people would calculate rationally what was in their own long-term interest, leading to greater general happiness.

Underlying Bentham's utilitarianism is a focus on the present and future. So the law should comprise statutes made by a democratic parliament based on reason, rather than hark back to custom and precedent; punishment and obedience to the state should be to prevent future harm, not retribution for past actions or dependent on past promises.

THE 'AUTO-ICON'

Seated inside a wooden cabinet at University College London for all to see is the skeleton of Jeremy Bentham, wearing his own clothes, with a wax head (it should have been the real one, but something went horribly wrong with the preservation process). This is Bentham's 'Auto-Icon', a man who is his own image, and he was preserved for the benefit of posterity, according to the terms of Bentham's will. Legend has it that the Auto-Icon regularly attends College Council meetings, going down on the minutes as 'present but not voting'.

∾∾

Georg Wilhelm Friedrich Hegel

(1770–1831)

WISE WORDS:

'What is rational is real and what is real is rational.'

— *The Philosophy of Right*

Born in Stuttgart, Georg Wilhelm Friedrich Hegel studied theology at Tübingen and worked as a tutor for some time before becoming a philosophy lecturer at Jena in 1801. Following Napoleon's victory at the Battle of Jena in 1806, however, the university was closed. The first of the four books published in Hegel's lifetime, *The Phenomenology of Spirit* (1807), appeared shortly afterwards, having been finished the day before the battle. During the nine years he then spent as a headmaster in Nuremberg, Hegel published his two-volume *Science of Logic* (1812 and 1816). In 1816, he became Professor of Philosophy at Heidelberg, where he wrote *The Encyclopedia of the Philosophical Sciences* (1817). His next appointment, in 1818, was as Professor of Philosophy in Berlin and it was here that he wrote *The Philosophy of Right* (1821). He stayed in Berlin until his death during a cholera epidemic.

Considered by many the greatest of the German idealist philosophers (see Kant, p.118), Hegel constructed a comprehensive system of thought to make sense of what he saw around him. The world, he says, is not a collection of separate, contradictory units; despite appearances, these contradictory units are in fact all parts of the unified whole – the Absolute – since they can be combined, refined and developed to produce a more perfect comprehension of reality. Reality must be rational, and its fundamental structure is mirrored in the structure of our thoughts as we strive to unify what at first seem to be contradictions. The stages we go through to arrive at logical truths must be the same as the stages by which reality progresses. Key to this progression is Hegel's concept of 'spirit', or mind, which by a dialectical process ultimately evolves into a higher form (see box).

In *The Phenomenology of Spirit*, Hegel outlines the mind's development from basic consciousness, via self-consciousness and reason, to the pure consciousness of spirit, which is absolute knowledge. In *The Science of Logic*, he explains how concepts of reality are revealed by dialectical reasoning: propose a thesis, consider its opposite or antithesis, and from the conflict between them a synthesis is born. This is the way in which human reasoning progresses, and it's not only logic that follows this progression; history too is moving in a similar way towards the Absolute, as his lecture notes (see below) make clear. In *The Encyclopedia of the Philosophical Sciences*, Hegel applies the dialectical approach to all areas of knowledge, while *The Philosophy of Right* contains his political philosophy.

Hegel's lecture notes on the philosophy of history – and also art, religion and philosophy – were published posthumously. He saw history as progress towards freedom: from the ancient empires of the East, where only rulers were free, via the Greeks with their devotion to the city-state, to the Protestant Reformation, when individuals realized they could achieve their own salvation.

Imbued with the spirit of his age, Hegel had confidence in concepts such as progress and purpose. He had enormous influence on German philosophy in the nineteenth century and, with his talk of historical progress, was central to the political theory of Karl Marx (see p.139), while his dialectical reasoning, minus the spirit, became Marx's dialectical materialism.

HEGELIAN TRIADS

Nothing to do with Chinese gangsters, these triads are the three parts of Hegel's dialectical process. To use his example: first take your thesis, *being*; then come up with its antithesis, *nothing*; the resulting synthesis is *becoming*. Simple: thesis and antithesis are reconciled in the concept 'becoming'.

❦

Arthur Schopenhauer

(1788–1860)

WISE WORDS:

'Every man takes the limits of his own field of vision for the limits of the world.'

— *Studies in Pessimism*

Arthur Schopenhauer was born in Danzig (now Gdansk in Poland), the son of a successful merchant who was a great devotee of the works of Voltaire (see p.109), and a mother with literary aspirations. When Prussia annexed the city in 1793, the family moved to Hamburg. Schopenhauer was sent to school in France and England, after which he returned home and, to please his father, became a clerk. However, he hated the commercial life, seeing himself more as an academic, and when his father committed suicide in 1805, leaving him a substantial inheritance, he was free to rethink his future.

By 1809, Schopenhauer was studying philosophy at the university in Göttingen. In 1811, he moved to Berlin to pursue his studies and he finally completed his dissertation in 1813 at Jena. Entitled 'On the Fourfold Root of the Principle of Sufficient Reason', it challenged the idea that what is real is what is rational – or, in other words, that the world is knowable; when his mother declared it unreadable, that was the end of their relationship. In 1814, Schopenhauer moved to Dresden, where he began work on his most famous book, *The World as Will and Representation* (1818). He became a lecturer at Berlin University in 1820 but had the temerity to timetable his lectures to coincide with those of Hegel (see p.127), whose work he despised. Unsurprisingly, since Hegel was the professor, Schopenhauer failed to attract many students, took umbrage and gave up his academic career to devote himself to writing.

For Schopenhauer, a declared atheist, the world is nothing but a series of momentary impressions, while the ultimate reality is the will – aimless, irrational, impenetrable and implacable. So the human intellect is trumped by blind striving that is doomed to disappoint. One of the first philosophers to be influenced by Eastern ideas – both Hindu and Buddhist – Schopenhauer insisted on the universality of suffering and held that salvation could be achieved only by overcoming the will through asceticism and renunciation. He identified three ways forward: studying philosophy; contemplating works of art and listening to music; and having compassion for others (since, beneath surface differences, we are all one). Among his later works, *On the Will in Nature* (1836) claims backing for his ideas from the empirical sciences, while *On the Basis of Morality* (1840) tackles such issues as freedom and determinism. In 1844, he published a revised edition of *The World as Will and Representation* with fifty additional chapters, thus almost doubling the size of the first edition, but it still did not make a big impression. It was only with the publication of *Parerga and Paralipomena* (1851), a late collection of philosophical essays and insights, that he finally received the attention he felt he deserved.

Though he tends to be billed as an out-and-out pessimist – and pessimism was very much to the fore in the aftermath of revolutionary upheavals in Europe at the time – Schopenhauer did suggest ways, especially through art, to transcend the frustrations of the human condition. For that reason, his ideas have appealed to numerous writers and musicians, such as Thomas Mann, Proust, Tolstoy and Wagner, as well as other philosophers, including Nietzsche (see p.144).

'OBIT ANUS, ABIT ONUS'

Although Schopenhauer declared that compassion was the main drive towards ethical behaviour, he doesn't seem to have been very driven in that direction himself. He was found guilty of kicking a seamstress down a flight of stairs and had to pay her a regular allowance in compensation. On her death he uttered the Latin words, *'Obit anus, abit onus'* – 'The old woman dies, the burden goes away.'

John Stuart Mill

(1806–73)

WISE WORDS:

'Bad men need nothing more to compass their ends, than that good men should look on and do nothing.'

– Inaugural address delivered at St Andrews University, 1867

Born in London, the son of the Scottish philosopher and historian James Mill, John Stuart Mill was a gifted child who was rigorously trained for greatness by his father. He studied Greek from the age of three; Latin came later, when he was all of eight, followed by logic and political economy in his early teens, and then history, law and philosophy. The idea was to equip the younger Mill to join the ranks of the Philosophical Radicals and champion the Benthamite cause (see box overleaf). For a while, all went according to plan and John Stuart Mill did as his father wished, helping to form the Utilitarian Society and contributing to the *Westminster Review*. In 1826, however, he had what he later referred to as a 'mental crisis' and from that time on became less of a hard-line utilitarian proselytizer.

Mill was a committed empiricist, convinced that truths could be obtained only from experience. He felt that the alternative – relying on intuition – simply reinforced existing prejudices. He wanted to produce a body of empirical knowledge that was as applicable to politics and morals as to the sciences. His first major work, the one that established his reputation as England's pre-eminent nineteenth-century philosopher, was *A System of Logic* (1843). The book details the principles of logic and mathematics, then discusses deduction and induction, observation and classification, fallacies of reasoning and the moral sciences. There was a clear practical dimension to all this, as Mill hoped his system would help to bring about social and political change.

The book for which he is best known, *On Liberty* (1859), discusses the freedom of the individual in relation to society and the state, arguing that 'the only purpose for which power can be rightfully exercised over any member of a civilized community, against his will, is to prevent harm to others. His own good, either physical or moral, is not a sufficient warrant.' Mill's position was not premised on ideas of rights but on a belief in utility: if everyone pursued their own happiness, together they would further the general good of society. The majority should not force out those who disagree with them and free speech should be encouraged, because genuine debate allows people to examine their convictions.

Utilitarianism (1863) proposes that there are objective standards of right and good, with good equating to the greatest happiness. Adding a twist on Jeremy Bentham, though, Mill distinguishes between higher and lower pleasures. Among his other works, *The Subjection of Women* (1869) develops his arguments for the freedom of the individual – 'the legal subordination of one sex to the other is wrong in itself ...' – and for the general good – '... and [is] now one of the chief hindrances to human improvement'.

THE PHILOSOPHICAL RADICALS

The name says it all: this was a group of radical thinkers inspired by the utilitarian philosophy of Jeremy Bentham (see p.123) and James Mill. Several, including for a short time John Stuart Mill, the latter's son, became Members of Parliament, where they used their influence to advocate political reform. The group's mouthpiece was the *Westminster Review*, a quarterly founded by Bentham and James Mill in 1823.

For thirty-five years, until it folded in 1858, John Stuart Mill worked for the East India Company, as his father had done before him. In 1865, he entered Parliament, where he was a strong advocate of women's rights, among other liberal concerns such as trade unionism and the abolition of slavery. Interestingly, he was the godfather of Bertrand Russell (see p.148).

⊚⊘

Søren Kierkegaard

(1813–55)

WISE WORDS:

'… knowledge has a relationship to the knower, who is essentially an existing individual, and [that] for this reason all essential knowledge is essentially related to existence.'

— *Concluding Unscientific Postscript to Philosophical Fragments*

Credited as the father of existentialism (see p.165), Søren Kierkegaard was born into an affluent family in Copenhagen. The youngest of seven children, he was brought up in a household dominated by his deeply religious and melancholic father, Michael, who believed he had been cursed by God as a child – he feared that none of his offspring would survive him and was indeed right about five of them. Kierkegaard studied theology at university in Copenhagen, but found himself increasingly drawn to philosophy and literature. A period of high living was followed by bouts of emotional turmoil and anguish. Having made a conscious decision to get a grip, he planned to become a cleric and to marry, but then in 1840 he broke off his engagement and abandoned all thoughts of a Church career. Instead, he would be an author. Over the next ten years, he wrote numerous books and pamphlets, including several major philosophical works. He often adopted pseudonyms, not to conceal his identity – he made no secret of it – but to allow him to take different standpoints.

Kierkegaard positioned himself firmly against the dominant German traditions of the day, in particular Hegel's contention that life could be explained by intellect alone. He saw this as a misguided attempt to replace God by elevating man, despite all the limitations on man's ability to make objective judgements. Instead he focused on the importance of the individual, stressing the centrality of the will and of free choice. For Kierkegaard, where human action and judgement were concerned, subjectivity was all. He carried his philosophical approach over into his works against organized Christianity, which he referred to disparagingly as Christendom. Here he again stressed individual choice as opposed to blind acceptance of the rituals of the Danish Lutheran Church.

In *Either/Or* (1843), Kierkegaard contrasts the aesthetic and the ethical ways of life. The former is all to do with immediate pleasure – whether sensory, physical or intellectual – while the latter is grounded in morality and the hereafter. Once people understand that the aesthetic path leads only to anxiety and despair, they will, he says, opt for the ethical. In *Fear and Trembling* (1843), he explains that, because God is essentially

ANGST

The English-speaking world has Kierkegaard to thank for introducing this word to describe the sense of profound insecurity and fear that haunts human beings. In Danish, *angst* means 'anxiety' or 'dread', and it was used by Kierkegaard in his book *The Concept of Anxiety* (1844) – also known as *The Concept of Dread*, depending on the translator. Kierkegaard believed that freedom of choice leaves people in a state of perpetual anxiety about their responsibilities to God. For later existentialists it was more a case of responsibilities to oneself, one's principles and other people.

unknowable, a leap of faith is necessary to move on from the ethical to the third – the religious – way, citing as an example Abraham's acceptance of God's order to sacrifice his beloved son Isaac. This 'teleological suspension of the ethical' demonstrates the ultimate in religious conviction and unconditional obedience to God's will. Kierkegaard was on a one-man mission to 'reintroduce Christianity into Christendom'.

It is in *Philosophical Fragments* (1844) and *Concluding Unscientific Postscripts to Philosophical Fragments* (1846) that Kierkegaard spells out his challenge to the Hegelian notion of a 'science of the spirit'. For him, 'subjectivity is truth', in contrast with Hegel's 'what is rational is real'.

The titles of other works such as *The Concept of Anxiety* (1844) and *The Sickness unto Death* (1849) reinforce Kierkegaard's image as the archetypal tormented, world-weary philosopher. His works were to exert great influence on those concerned with problems of religion and ethics, most especially the existentialists among them.

CAPITALISM AND COMMUNISM

Capitalism, according to Progress Publishers of Moscow, is a 'socio-economic formulation … based on private ownership of the means of production and the exploitation of wage labour … The class struggle of the proletariat, which pervades the entire history of capitalism, ends in the socialist revolution.'

Which leads us swiftly on to communism: 'a classless social system with one form of public ownership of the means of production and full social equality of all members of society; under it … all the springs of co-operative wealth will flow more abundantly, and the great principle, "From each according to his ability, to each according to his needs", will be implemented' (*A Dictionary of Philosophy*, 1967).

Sounds so simple, doesn't it?

◎◎

Karl Marx

(1818–83)

WISE WORDS:

'The philosophers have only interpreted the world in various ways. The point however is to change it.'

– 'Eleventh Thesis on Feuerbach' and on Marx's tombstone in Highgate Cemetery, London

Karl Marx was born and brought up in Trier, a cosmopolitan Prussian city, by parents who had converted from Judaism to avoid anti-Semitism. Having studied law at Bonn for a year, in 1836 he moved to Berlin, where his interest in philosophy developed under the influence of the Young Hegelians, a group that opposed the idealist teachings of Hegel in favour of materialism but made use of Hegel's dialectical method (see overleaf).

In 1842, Marx started editing the liberal Cologne-based *Rheinische Zeitung*, but it was suppressed by the government the following year and he moved to Paris. Here he became a communist and met Friedrich Engels, who was to be a lifelong friend. Marx left France for political reasons in 1845 and went to Brussels, where he collaborated with Engels on *German Ideology* (1845–6), which introduced Marx's 'materialist conception of history', and the famous *Communist Manifesto* (1848), which needs no introduction. After revolutionary turmoil in Paris in 1848, he returned to Cologne to edit the *Neue Rheinische Zeitung*, a more radical version of his old paper. When that too was closed down in 1849, he moved to London, where he lived for the rest of his life.

In the reading room of the British Museum, Marx began work on *Capital* (1867), one of the most influential books of all time. It contains his definitive views on the theory of surplus value (i.e. profits made by capitalists) and the exploitation of the working classes, and anticipates the overthrow of capitalism by socialism and the emergence of a classless communist society. The philosophical underpinnings of these ideas were historical and dialectical materialism.

If eighteenth-century materialism is the doctrine that nothing exists except matter, historical materialism is Marx's new take: the application of dialectical methods to historical evolution, showing among other things that humans have, through the ages, entered into – and been defined by – social contracts designed to maintain production of the necessities of life. A division of labour coupled with a division of society into classes – whether slaves and masters or workers and capitalists – is historically how humans have organized and sustained themselves.

The ideas first outlined in *German Ideology* – humans are different from other animals because they produce what they need to survive; what they are depends on how and what they produce; their nature is conditioned by their material conditions – were expanded in *Contribution to the Critique of Political Economy* (1859): 'It is not the consciousness of men that determines their existence, but, on the contrary, their social existence that determines their consciousness.'

Which leads on to dialectical materialism. Marx contrasts his dialectic method to Hegel's: 'To Hegel … the process of thinking, which, under the name of "the Idea", he even transforms into an independent subject, is the demiurgos of the real world, and the real world is only the external, phenomenal form of "the Idea". With me … the ideal is nothing else than the material world reflected by the human mind, and translated into forms of thought.'

As Marx saw it, each stage of society generated forces that would bring it down, with a new society emerging from the conflict: thesis/antithesis/synthesis.

Marx took philosophy out into the real world, with all its political and economic complexities. Though many of his doctrines have had terrible practical consequences – think Stalin's Russia, Mao's China – the idea that the economy prompts historical change is still influential regardless of the political side of Marxism.

A PRAGMATIC DUO

The word 'pragmatism' was introduced into philosophy by the American Charles Peirce (1839–1914), who formulated his pragmatic maxim to clarify the meaning of any given concept: 'Consider what effects, which might conceivably have practical bearings, we conceive the object of our conception to have. Then, our conception of these effects is the whole of our conception of the object' ('How to Make Our Ideas Clear', *Popular Science Monthly*, Vol. 12, 1878). Perhaps realizing that this clarification wasn't terribly clear,

---

Peirce paraphrased the maxim thus: 'We must look to the upshot of our concepts in order rightly to apprehend them.' So pragmatism was not so much a philosophical system as a theory of meaning.

A scientist by training, although he did lecture in logic for five years at Johns Hopkins University in Baltimore, Peirce believed that concepts need to be tested in the way that scientific hypotheses are. Just as we analyse scientific ideas by looking at the effects they have and the way we can make use of them, so the truth of a theory – and the truth can only ever be provisional, never certain – is inseparable from its consequences. For Peirce, 'The opinion which is fated to be ultimately agreed to by all who investigate, is what we mean by the truth, and the object represented in this opinion is the real. That is the way I would explain reality' (*Collected Papers*, Vol. 5, 1935). Or: once we've all agreed that something is true, it becomes our reality. He felt obliged to coin the word pragmaticism for his own distinctive approach once his compatriot William James (1842–1910), brother of the novelist Henry James, started to expand pragmatism's application beyond Peirce's theory of meaning.

James, a graduate of Harvard Medical School, where he also taught for a while, soon turned his attention to philosophy and psychology, and became a professor in both disciplines. His 1,200-page *Principles of Psychology* (1890), which is credited with laying the foundations of the subject as it is studied to this day – with its combined emphasis on scientific, lab-based experimental work and the importance of direct experience – was grounded in functionalism: things being understood by their function.

Taking Peirce's ideas further, James argued that if a concept means literally what you do with it, then its truth must consist in doing whatever it is successfully. Ideas, just like minds, he was sure, can be studied by their function. In *Pragmatism* (1907), his best-known philosophical work, James states, 'If you follow the pragmatic method … you must bring out of each word its practical cash-value [he means its usefulness to us], set it at work within the stream of your experience.' Concepts are part of an active process, not just static things to be examined. He turned meaning into action: '"The true", to put it very briefly, is only the expedient in the way of our thinking, just as "the right" is only the expedient in the way of our behaving.' In other words, what's true is simply what results in a useful processing of experience; what's right is what helps in dealing with experience.

Friedrich Nietzsche

(1844–1900)

WISE WORDS:

'What I understand by "philosopher": a terrible explosive in the presence of which everything is in danger.'

— *Ecce Homo*

Born in the province of Saxony, the son of a Lutheran pastor, Nietzsche was a brilliant student during his time at school and the universities of Bonn and Leipzig. At Bonn, he studied theology and philology, with a view to becoming a pastor, too, but once he lost his faith that route was closed to him. He moved to Leipzig to concentrate on philology and it was here that he came across a copy of Schopenhauer's *The World as Will and Representation* (see p.129). From that moment, he was a convert. He became Professor of Philology at the University of Basel in 1869, aged only twenty-four. For a short time in 1870, he was a medical orderly in the Franco-Prussian War, from which he returned in bad health. This was the start of a long decline, both physical and mental, that forced him to resign from the university in 1878 and left him insane from 1889 until his death.

Nietzsche wasn't the conventional sort of philosopher, labouring methodically to construct a new theory about the nature of knowledge. Instead he ranged widely over questions of morality and religion in a number of intensely written works that ponder what makes human beings act they way they do. Freud later expressed amazement that what he called Nietzsche's premonitions and insights often tallied with the results of lengthy psychoanalysis.

In his first book, *The Birth of Tragedy* (1872), Nietzsche compares 'Apollonian' and 'Dionysian' values in ancient Greece – order and reason vs. primal instincts – concerned that the importance of the latter has been overlooked and seeing much to admire in the heroic qualities of Homer's warriors.

Essays and books of aphorisms followed, in which Nietzsche identifies fear and the striving for power as key motivators: the 'will to power', he goes on to claim, is the fundamental human drive. In *Thus Spoke Zarathustra* (1883) and *Beyond Good and Evil* (1886), he proposes a new life-affirming morality based on confident self-assertion. The will to power is embodied in his *Übermensch* ('superman'), who is strong enough to break free from conventional morality, control his passions and direct his energies towards creativity: this is 'master-morality'. Rather than wait for an imaginary afterlife, the superman lives fully in the here and now.

The will to power went hand in hand with Nietzsche's virulent opposition to Christianity, which was nothing but a denial of the life-affirming passions. Christianity promoted the weak and the downtrodden, encouraging a 'slave-morality' that had no place in his brave new world. For Nietzsche, developments in science and secular reasoning had undermined religion – indeed, killed it off: 'God is dead,' he had already announced. Now the universal perspective given by God had gone, people would follow their own values, with ethics grounded in human existence rather than divine revelation.

Nietzsche feared that Europe would sink into nihilism without a new morality. He rejected democracy, 'bourgeois' values and utilitarian ethics – more slave stuff. Happiness and 'the greater good' were feeble goals, lacking the life-affirming qualities of the masters: power, wealth, strength and health – all things Nietzsche was signally lacking by the end of his life. And it did his reputation no good at all when the Nazis absorbed his 'superman' into their ideology of a master race.

MODERN TIMES

◎◎

It hardly seems necessary to mention wars again, but all that budding European nationalism in the nineteenth century was bound to end in tears. The First World War well and truly swept away the certainties of the Victorian era, and the political fallout significantly altered the map of Europe. The economic consequences in both America and Europe followed a path of boom and bust that's oh so familiar today, while also contributing to the outbreak of the Second World War, with all the horrors that entailed.

In the philosophical world, another war was declared, as the lines were drawn between the Anglo-American (or analytical) school and the Continentals. In the former camp were philosophers such as Russell, Moore and Wittgenstein, who relied on mathematical logic and linguistic analysis to isolate and then deal with discrete philosophical questions. Ranged against them were the likes of Heidegger, Sartre, Foucault and Derrida, who saw philosophy as inseparable from its historical background, developing their theories of existentialism, structuralism and post-structuralism, which seemed like so much obfuscation to the analytical establishment.

Of course, it now turns out that this was only a phoney war, with plenty of overlaps, but the distinctions hold true in general terms.

ᗗᗖ

Bertrand Russell

(1872–1970)

WISE WORDS:

'Mathematics, rightly viewed, possesses not only truth, but supreme beauty – a beauty cold and austere, like that of sculpture.'

– 'The Study of Mathematics'

Born in Trelleck, Monmouthshire, into an aristocratic family, Bertrand Russell was orphaned by the age of four and was brought up by his grandmother, the widow of the Liberal statesman Lord John Russell, first Earl Russell (Bertrand eventually inherited the title himself, becoming third Earl Russell in 1931). He was educated at home, studying modern languages, economics, constitutional history, mathematics and science – rather than Greek and Latin, as would have been more usual for someone of his background – and this laid the foundations for his wide-ranging intellectual interests. In 1890, he went up to Trinity College, Cambridge, to read mathematics, switching to philosophy in 1893 and graduating with first-class honours the following year. He became a fellow in

1895, shortly after getting married. On returning from his honeymoon in Berlin, Russell wrote *German Social Democracy* (1896), a political study that was the first of his many books. Around the same time, he encountered the work of a group of German mathematicians who, by analysing the fundamental concepts of mathematics, were trying to provide it with logically coherent foundations. For Russell, their ideas had significance not only for mathematics but also for philosophy: if mathematical truth could be proved objectively, why not the truth about human knowledge, too?

Rejecting the Hegelian idealist philosophy that he had so far espoused, with its quest for overarching systems (see p.127), Russell focused instead on in-depth logical analysis. In *Principles of Mathematics* (1903), he argued that maths should be treated as a subset of logic, while the three-volume *Principia Mathematica* (1910–13), which he wrote with Alfred North Whitehead, reinforced the idea of the logical derivation of mathematics, with additional philosophical analysis that demonstrated how everyday language and grammar were not always clear enough to convey true logical forms. This built on an earlier essay, 'On Denoting' (1905), in which Russell highlighted the philosophical problems raised by the slipperiness of language in relation to naming and describing objects: how was it possible to speak meaningfully of non-existent things (Russell gives as an example 'the present King of France') or even things that can't possibly exist ('the round square', as in 'the round square is a contradiction')?

His answer was to keep things as simple as possible – à la William of Ockham (see p.80) – by subjecting the meaning of words and how they are used to the same sort of rigorous analysis that would be used on mathematical concepts. This analytical approach – Russell was one of the founders of analytic philosophy – led away from the search for grand metaphysical systems towards the study of linguistics and logical positivism, not to mention atomism (see pp.177 and 175).

Russell was renowned for his ability to convey complex ideas to a general audience, with books on such subjects as science, politics, ethics and educational theory, plus mathematics and philosophy, selling in quantities that can only be dreamed of

A POLITICAL ANIMAL

Bertrand Russell was unsuccessful in the May 1907 Wimbledon by-election as the candidate for the National Union of Women's Suffrage Societies. Three years later, he was asked to represent the Liberals in Bedford but decided against it. In 1922, he stood for the Labour Party in Chelsea, but again failed to win a seat in Parliament. A committed pacifist throughout the First World War, Russell went to prison for his beliefs in 1918. After the Second World War, he was outspoken on the subject of nuclear disarmament, playing a leading role in CND, and in 1961, when nearly ninety years old, was imprisoned for his part in a sit-down protest in Whitehall.

today. His *History of Western Philosophy* appeared in 1945 and has been in print ever since.

An enthusiastic communicator, Russell took part in many radio broadcasts for the BBC during the 1940s and 1950s, and in 1950 was awarded the Nobel Prize for Literature. He remained active as a political campaigner for most of his long life, retiring to Wales only towards the very end.

෨෨

G. E. Moore

(1873–1958)

WISE WORDS:

'All moral laws ... are merely statements that certain kinds of actions will have good effects.'

– Principia Ethica

Born in London, G. E. Moore was educated at Dulwich College and then Trinity College, Cambridge. He was originally reading classics, but once he became friendly with Bertrand Russell (see p.148) he switched to philosophy. After graduating, Moore spent some time studying on his own before returning to Cambridge in 1911 to lecture in philosophy. He was Professor of Mental Philosophy and Logic from 1925 to 1939, at which point he was succeeded by Ludwig Wittgenstein (see p.156). He also edited the influential philosophy journal *Mind* from 1921 to 1944.

As he wrote in the autobiographical *Philosophy of G. E. Moore* (1942), Moore was puzzled in his early career not so much by the world or the sciences, but by the things other philosophers had said about them. Like Russell, he found he could not sustain his initial fascination with Hegelian idealism (see p.127), deciding it just made no sense, and so he moved towards a simpler, more analytical approach. This he expounded first in his article 'The Refutation of Idealism', which appeared in *Mind* in 1903, and then in later works such as *In Defence of Common Sense* (1925) and *Proof of an External World* (1939). He started from the position that no sensible person could disagree that a large body of shared beliefs about the world existed and that these could be expressed as straightforward propositions, the meanings of which were not only perfectly clear but also palpably true.

All of which meant, Moore felt, that earlier philosophers must have been mistaken either about the nature of philosophy or in their approach towards it. Why did they agonize over problems of meaning, when there were none, or over the truth of propositions, as that was beyond doubt, too? According to Moore, this left just one thing for philosophers to do: analyse these straightforward propositions to extract their significance.

His *Principia Ethica* (1903) considers what's known as the naturalistic fallacy – the confusion between natural attribution and moral definition – with a view to analysing the fundamental moral question 'What is goodness?' You cannot, Moore says, define 'good' in terms of, say, happiness, because that just raises another question: 'Is happiness always good?' Other properties

BLOOMSBURY CONNECTIONS

While at Trinity, Russell and Moore joined the select discussion group the Cambridge Apostles. Among other Apostles were Roger Fry, John Maynard Keynes, E. M. Forster and Lytton Strachey, all of whom were to play a major role in the Bloomsbury Group.

That much-biographied happy band, which included Clive and Vanessa Bell and Virginia Woolf, met regularly from around 1905 to 1930 in Bloomsbury, central London. Fry became best known as an art critic, Keynes as an economist, Forster a novelist and Strachey a biographer and critic. Their discussions on aesthetic and philosophical issues, not to mention their behaviour, were heavily influenced by Moore's *Principia Ethica* (1903) and Whitehead and Russell's *Principia Mathematica* (1910–13), which led them to come up with their own definitions of the good, the true and the beautiful, challenging the received ideas – for which read the artistic, social and sexual restrictions – of Victorian society.

can be attributed to 'good', but they too only illustrate it rather than define it. Moore concludes that goodness is a simple, unanalysable quality, known simply by intuition. The best we can do is to ask what *things* are good, and here he had no hesitation in providing the answer: friendship and aesthetic experience. No wonder he was so popular with the Bloomsbury Group (see box on previous page).

❧

Martin Heidegger

(1889–1976)

WISE WORDS:

'The most thought-provoking thing in our thought-provoking time is that we are still not thinking.'

— *What is Called Thinking?*

Born in Messkirch, Baden, the son of a Catholic sexton, Martin Heidegger joined the Jesuits as a novice after leaving school but abandoned the idea a month later. Instead he went to Freiburg University to study theology, switching later to philosophy. He started lecturing in philosophy there in 1915, was appointed professor at Marburg in 1923 and then returned to Freiburg as professor in 1928. He became rector in 1933, joining the Nazi Party shortly afterwards, and in his inaugural address, 'The Role of the University in the New Reich', expressed support for Hitler and his aims – which is the first thing people tend to remember about Heidegger today.

His most important work, the unfinished – and some

would say unfinishable – *Being and Time* (1927), introduces the topic that resonates through much of his later writings: the 'question of being' (*Seinsfrage*). Rather than simply take for granted what it means for someone to 'be', Heidegger felt it was necessary to unpick the metaphysical models used by earlier philosophers from Aristotle onwards. As far as he could see, metaphysics does not reveal anything about the true nature of being; instead, all that really exists is people's consciousness of their own place in the world, or of what the world means to them (their 'being-there' or *Dasein*). This then brings in the time angle of the book's title. Because life is finite, humans must remain constantly aware of the inevitability of their own death in order to live authentically. They are free to choose their actions and focus their energies within the world they have been born into: the possibilities do not stop until death.

Heidegger was troubled by the sense that modern technology was divorcing people from what he called the 'nearness and shelter' of being, making life 'inauthentic' in a way that had not been true for their more primitive ancestors, who had lived in happy communion with nature.

All of this opens the way to some of the major themes of twentieth-century history and thought: individual freedom, one's place in the world, authenticity, angst, guilt and destiny. The Second World War was on the horizon, while such existentialists as Jean-Paul Sartre (see p.164) and deconstructionists as Jacques Derrida (see p.172) were waiting in the wings.

◎◎

Ludwig Wittgenstein
(1889–1951)

WISE WORDS:

'Whereof one cannot speak, thereof one must be silent.'

— *Tractatus Logico-Philosophicus*

The youngest of eight children, Ludwig Wittgenstein was born in Vienna into a wealthy and cultured family. His father was a hugely successful industrialist, a great music lover and an art collector; Wittgenstein was intended to be the practical member of the family. From 1906 to 1908, he studied mechanical engineering in Berlin. He then went to Manchester University, where he became fascinated by mathematics, so in 1911, he moved to Cambridge to study mathematical logic with Bertrand Russell (see p.148). After two years, Russell declared that he had taught Wittgenstein all he could. While Russell's interest was uncovering the logical foundations of mathematics, Wittgenstein wanted to fathom the foundations of logic itself. At the start of the First World War, he joined the Austrian army, but for the next four years he worked on what was to become *Tractatus Logico-Philosophicus* (1922), the only book published in his lifetime.

In a preface written in 1918, Wittgenstein boldly declared, 'I therefore believe myself to have found, on all essential points, the final solution of the problems' – as in the problems of philosophy. It was all a question of language – specifically, its nature and limitations.

The world is made up of discrete 'atomic' facts, from which larger facts can be built. Language, the purpose of which is to state the facts, is similarly made up of 'atomic' propositions, from which larger propositions can be built. Language and thought together create a picture of the state of affairs to which they refer. To be meaningful, language must comprise propositions that are pictures of the facts the world is composed of; it must refer to the real. Which makes a great deal of speculative philosophy, not to mention value judgements, literally meaningless. And if the limits of language are also the limits of thought ... well, see the quotation at the start of this entry. Having devised this logically coherent scheme, thanks to which no one need ever talk nonsense again, Wittgenstein felt he'd reached the end of the line with philosophy and started to look for a new career. But it turned out that this was just the end of philosophy phase one.

Wittgenstein had inherited a fortune when his father died in 1913, and he now gave it away, opting from 1920 for the life of a schoolteacher in rural Austria instead. When this experiment failed, he turned his hand to architecture, building a house for one of his sisters in Vienna. While there, in 1929, he met members of the Vienna Circle (see box overleaf), who were busy developing the ideas of the *Tractatus* into the rigorous tenets of logical positivism. Their activities must have persuaded Wittgenstein that philosophy still held more challenges, because he returned to Cambridge that year, first as a fellow of Trinity College and then, from 1939 to 1947, as Professor of

Philosophy. Here his work took a new turn, summarized in *Philosophical Investigations* (1953), which seems to reject most of what was said in the *Tractatus*.

THE VIENNA CIRCLE

This group of academics at Vienna University in the 1920s and 1930s were known as logical positivists – or logical empiricists – because their interest in the sciences and mathematics led them to identify mathematical logic as the way to handle philosophical problems.

Wittgenstein's *Tractatus Logico-Philosophicus* was of enormous influence, although he did not join the group. In 1929, they produced a pamphlet outlining their basic tenets: knowledge comes from experience (the positivist/empiricist bit) and philosophical problems must be clarified before they can be tackled (that's logical), with propositions that can't be verified dismissed as meaningless (no more discussions of ethics, religion and aesthetics). Their influence soon spread beyond the German-speaking world, but within a few years the group had dispersed because of Nazi hostility and the onset of the war.

In this later work, Wittgenstein no longer sees language as a static, logical system; it is now a means of communicating and furthering social functions in the real world, and therefore something that changes according to context. He identifies what he calls 'language games' – different sorts of language with different uses – that each have their own rules but come together to make up a toolkit for philosophers. Clarity can only come by acknowledging this diversity. For Wittgenstein, by the end, the aim seems to be to use language to untangle the linguistic tangles philosophers have made, thus doing away with problems rather than needing to solve them.

❦

Gilbert Ryle

(1900–1976)

WISE WORDS:

'the dogma of the ghost in the machine [referring to Cartesian dualism].'

— *The Concept of Mind*

Born in Brighton, Gilbert Ryle studied at Oxford and started lecturing in philosophy there in 1924. Having worked in intelligence during the Second World War, he returned to Oxford in 1945 to become Waynflete Professor of Metaphysical Philosophy at Magdalen College, a position he held until his retirement in 1968. From 1947 until 1971, following in the footsteps of G. E. Moore (see p.151), he was also the editor of *Mind*.

An advocate of linguistic analysis, or the 'ordinary language' school of philosophy, Ryle felt that his job as a philosopher was to root out 'the sources in linguistic idioms of recurrent misconceptions and absurd theories'. As far as he could see, errors and confusion in philosophy came about when expressions that clearly belonged to one logical category were treated as if they belonged to another: what he refers to as category mistakes. The example often cited is taken from his major work, *The Concept of Mind* (1949): 'She came home in a flood of tears and a sedan-chair.' Though this is a perfectly well-turned sentence from a syntactical point of view, it is also absurd in that it is treating a state of mind and a material object as if they were one and the same. Ryle's idea is that, by pushing expressions to the limits of absurdity in this way, philosophical problems can be exposed and dealt with.

This is the method he uses in the same book to dismantle what he calls the 'official doctrine' of philosophy: Cartesian dualism (see p.94) – the separation of mind and body. For Ryle, this was the category mistake to end all category mistakes, and it stemmed from the fact that Descartes did not have our knowledge of biology. Ryle can see no logical reason for treating the mind as some sort of ghostly entity to be tacked on to the human body, which is acknowledged to exist in space and is subject to physical laws. Rather, mental concepts such as emotions, sensations, self-knowledge, imagination and the intellect should be seen as innate human dispositions to behave in certain ways in certain circumstances – in other words, there is no split between mind and body.

Throughout his career, Ryle wrote widely not just on the philosophy of language but also on epistemology (the study of knowledge) and the history of philosophy, and it was his influence that helped put Oxford at the centre of philosophical study in the UK after the war.

Karl Popper

(1902–94)

WISE WORDS:

'… it is very hard to learn from very big mistakes.'
— *The Open Society and Its Enemies*

Karl Popper was born into an affluent family in Vienna, capital of the Austro-Hungarian Empire, and went to university there in 1918. He briefly became a Marxist, but resisted the mental straitjacket he felt historical materialism imposed. By the time he graduated in 1922, the empire had been dismembered in the wake of the First World War and his family had lost all their money. However, Vienna remained an intellectual centre, home to the psychiatrists Sigmund Freud and Alfred Adler, as well as the logical positivists of the Vienna Circle (see p.158), whose interest in the natural sciences Popper shared. He worked as a schoolteacher from 1930, but emigrated to New Zealand in 1937, worried by the prospect of German occupation. He lectured in philosophy at Canterbury University College, Christchurch, until 1945, when he moved to the London School of Economics. There he was Professor of Logic and Scientific Method from 1949 until 1969.

Popper's main interests were the philosophy of science and political philosophy. Though he was associated with the Vienna Circle, his early work argues that philosophical problems can't be tackled through an analysis of language or meaning; nor does he consider science more verifiable than metaphysics. In *The Logic of Scientific Discovery* (1934), he challenges the idea that science is a process of induction, with theories coming from repeated observations and proved by experiment. Further, he claims that it's actually impossible to verify a scientific theory since no amount of observation can show beyond doubt that a hypothesis is true, while only one observation is needed to refute it. Which makes falsification the way to go.

Popper distinguishes between science, which generates theories leading to empirical predictions that can be jettisoned when the experiment fails, and non-science. The theories of Freud, Adler and Marx fall into the latter camp, as psychiatry cannot generate empirical predictions and Marxism is never knocked off course by observational disproof. It is with true science – the theories of Einstein, say – that hypotheses can be proved wrong if a single observation goes against them. Eliminating falsified theories leaves only objective scientific knowledge, which corresponds to the truth.

WITTGENSTEIN'S POKER

In 1946, Karl Popper delivered a lecture to the Cambridge University Moral Science Club entitled 'Are There Philosophical Problems?' His contention that there were incensed at least one listener, Ludwig Wittgenstein (see p.156), who believed that philosophy had no right to concern itself with such issues, being all a question of language. For ten minutes their tussle was purely verbal, until Wittgenstein picked up a poker and started waving it around. In Popper's version of events, the confrontation ended when Wittgenstein asked for an example of a moral rule and Popper came up with, 'Not to threaten visiting lecturers with pokers' – at which point Wittgenstein dropped the offending object and stalked off. Of course, this is just Popper's version ...

As for Popper's political philosophy, in *The Open Society and Its Enemies* (1945) and *The Poverty of Historicism* (1957), he disputes the idea that history has inevitable outcomes, seeing this as simply another untestable, unscientific assertion to justify the actions of fanatics and oppressors – he challenges the views of Plato, Hegel and Marx (see pp.35, 127 and 139) in this respect. History, he says, will always be affected by future discoveries that no one can possibly know about, and political actions,

however well intentioned, will always have unforeseen consequences. So, instead, he makes a heartfelt plea for open,
democratic societies that go in for a bit of gentle 'social engineering' as and when necessary.

Jean-Paul Sartre

(1905–80)

WISE WORDS:

'Man, being condemned to be free, carries the weight
of the whole world on his shoulders; he is responsible
for the world and for himself as a way of being.'

– Being and Nothingness

Born and educated in Paris, where he attended the prestigious
Ecole Normale Supérieure – as Foucault and Derrida (see
pp.169 and 172) would also do – Jean-Paul Sartre started teaching philosophy in Le Havre in 1931. Having been awarded a
grant to study at the French Institute in Berlin, he spent 1934
and 1935 pursuing his interest in the work of contemporary
German philosophers, especially Heidegger (see p.154). When
he returned to France, Sartre taught in Le Havre, Laon and
Paris, and also published his first novel, *Nausea* (1938).
Conscripted at the outbreak of the Second World War, he was
captured by the Germans in June 1940 and sent to a prisoner-
of-war camp. Not one to let these things get him down, he ran

classes for fellow inmates on the work of Heidegger. Following his release in spring 1941, he taught in Paris for the rest of the war and was also active in the French Resistance. Once hostilities were over, he abandoned academia in favour of writing for a wider audience and active political engagement.

Sartre is synonymous with existentialism, the principles of which he defined in his philosophical writings, embodied in his plays and novels, and lived out to the end of his life. This extract from his 1946 lecture 'Existentialism is a Humanism' is worth quoting at length: 'Atheistic existentialism, of which I am a representative, declares ... that if God does not exist there is at least one being whose existence comes before its essence, a being which exists before it can be defined by any conception of it. That being is man or, as Heidegger has it, the human reality. What do we mean by saying that existence precedes essence? We mean that man first of all exists, encounters himself, surges up in the world – and defines himself afterwards. If man as the existentialist sees him is not definable, it is because to begin with he is nothing. He will not be anything until later, and then he will be what he makes of himself. Thus, there is no human nature, because there is no God to have a conception of it. Man simply is ... That is the first principle of existentialism.'

In the earlier *Being and Nothingness* (1943), Sartre had already explored the problem at the heart of existentialism: if we are all ultimately alone, each of us responsible for what we make of ourselves – 'condemned to be free' – how can we relate to other people and things in the world? He saw two options. Either we passively accept the status quo, operating as mere objects, or we challenge the current situation and aspire to something better. But that just leads to another question: in a world in which we have no allegiance except to ourselves, how is moral action or political commitment possible?

Sartre attempts to provide answers through plays such as *No Exit* (1944) and novels such as the *Roads to Freedom* trilogy (1945–9). As he made clear in *What is Literature?* (1947), he saw writing not as an activity for its own sake, a simple description of characters and situations, but as a way to tackle issues relating to human freedom. Literature must be committed, since artistic creation is a moral activity. This means writers have a duty to participate in social and political issues, which explains Sartre's involvement with Marxism and then the radical New Left in France.

◎◎

A. J. Ayer

(1910–89)

WISE WORDS:

'The criterion which we use to test the genuineness of apparent statements of fact is the criterion of verifiability.'

— *Language, Truth and Logic*

Born in London and educated at Eton and Oxford, Alfred Jules Ayer was a pupil of Gilbert Ryle (see p.159). He worked in intelligence during the Second World War and then, in 1946, after a period in Paris as attaché at the British Embassy, became Grote Professor of the Philosophy of Mind and Logic at University College, London, a position he held until 1959. He moved to Oxford that year, having been appointed Wykeham Professor of Logic.

During the 1930s, Ayer had attended meetings of the Vienna Circle (see p.158) and in his first book, *Language, Truth and Logic* (1936), he presents the classic English version of logical positivism. He makes it clear that there are only two types of knowledge: knowledge that is empirically verifiable (it can be tested by observation) and knowledge that is analytic (it is true by definition, according to linguistic rules). Scientific statements and statements of everyday fact are examples of the former, while mathematical statements and statements of logic are examples of the latter. Ayer takes the argument further by saying that, if propositions fall into *neither* camp, they must be devoid of meaning, boiling down to mere expressions of personal opinion. To this category he consigns religious and metaphysical statements such as 'God exists' – or, equally, 'God does not exist' – as well as the idea that there is a realm of things out there, existing beyond phenomena.

In *The Problem of Knowledge* (1956) and also in his 1972–3 Gifford Lectures, delivered at the University of St Andrews and then published as *The Central Questions of Philosophy* (1973), Ayer reiterates the idea that the role of the philosopher is to use logic to clarify the basic concepts of science, not to come up with schemes – whether based on metaphysics or theology – that provide great insights into how things really are.

A. J. AYER KNOCKS OUT MIKE TYSON

According to Ben Rogers in his 1989 biography of Ayer, a couple of years earlier the philosopher had been at a New York party hosted by fashion designer Fernando Sánchez. When someone asked for help because her friend was being assaulted, Ayer went to see what was happening and found the boxer Mike Tyson pestering a young Naomi Campbell, then at the start of her modelling career. Ayer promptly told Tyson to stop, but the boxer just rounded on him, saying, 'Do you know who the fuck I am? I'm the heavyweight champion of the world.' To which Ayer replied, 'And I am the former Wykeham Professor of Logic. We are both pre-eminent in our field; I suggest that we talk about this like rational men.' Which is what they did, while Ms Campbell quietly slipped away.

◎◎

Michel Foucault

(1926–84)

WISE WORDS:

'What is philosophy today ... if it does not consist in, instead of legitimizing what we already know, undertaking to know how and how far it might be possible to think otherwise?'

— *The Use of Pleasure*

Born and raised in Poitiers, Michel Foucault went to Paris after the Second World War, where he attended the Ecole Normale Supérieure. In addition to studying philosophy he developed a great interest in psychology after a period of acute depression, briefly teaching the subject at Lille University. After spending some time abroad, he returned to France and started lecturing in philosophy, first at Clermont-Ferrand and then at Vincennes, before becoming Professor of the History of Systems of Thought at the Collège de France in Paris in 1970.

Foucault drew on his interest in history, philosophy, psychology and linguistics to analyse the relationship between history at large and the history of thought. He did not see how history could be treated as a unified process capable of revealing objective truths or coming up with universally applicable lessons, since the knowledge available to people in any given historical period is bound to be conditioned by existing social norms, forms of cultural expression, the ways language is used and the prevailing philosophies of the time: in other words, systems of thought. Seen in this light, it's clear that what counts as 'normal' for human beings is fluid, determined by different factors at different times.

To get at the concepts that underpin these systems of thought, Foucault adopted what he called an 'archaeological' approach. Choosing specific historical periods within which to work, he studied often overlooked areas – psychiatry, medicine, punishment systems, sexual behaviour – to uncover the conditions that make certain practices, institutions and theories possible.

As far as Foucault was concerned, it all came down to power, which could be looked at through the prism of those whom society chooses to exclude: the insane, prisoners, sexual deviants. In *Madness and Civilization* (1961), he claims that Enlightenment 'reason' packaged up madness and consigned it to the asylum, while *The Birth of the Clinic* (1963) treats medical understanding in a similar way. Things billed as progressive and humane advances in treatment were, he says, just aspects of social and political control. By looking at prisons, *Discipline and Punish* (1975) demonstrates how the meaning of punishment can change over time, while *The Will to Knowledge* (1976), the first of a projected six-volume *History of Sexuality*, only three of which were published, discusses the centrality of one's sexual identity.

Foucault is not saying that power and freedom are incompatible, or that power is automatically a bad thing – it's simply a fact of life. But the idea that freedom is something objective that can be protected by the state is a fallacy, as his studies of history make clear. Likewise, the suggestion that truth can be found through the pursuit of rationality is just another historical invention. The search for truth, especially the truth about ourselves, remains valid, but there are no easy answers. The role of philosophy is to help us to think through the hard ones, in other words, the previously unarticulated thoughts.

A LINGUISTIC SPEAKS

Professor Noam Chomsky (1928–), who has been teaching at the Massachusetts Institute of Technology since 1955, started a revolution in linguistic analysis and in doing so contributed to the great rationalist vs. empiricist debate that had been going on for three centuries, since Descartes and Locke (see pp.92 and 96).

In his *Syntactic Structures* (1957), he challenged the then accepted view that children acquire language through instruction and experience. For Chomsky, the speed with which it is mastered suggested that there must be an innate predisposition for language within children. He took this to mean that an unlearned, universal grammar exists, supplying rules that can be recognized immediately whatever the language encountered. Within his system, there are two levels of linguistic knowledge: deep structures, which refer to

---

the universal grammar shared by all languages, and surface structures, which cover specific words and sounds used in a particular language. To Chomsky's mind, we are all born hard-wired for language and his *Cartesian Linguistics* (1966) reiterates the rationalist – and therefore anti-empiricist – implications of this idea.

∞

Jacques Derrida

(1930–2004)

WISE WORDS:

'There is nothing outside of the text.'

– Of Grammatology

Born in Algiers, Jacques Derrida studied at the Ecole Normale Supérieure in Paris and taught there for twenty years, from 1964, after a stint teaching philosophy at the Sorbonne. Renowned as the founder of deconstruction, his work was initially seen as relevant only in the field of literary criticism – where texts can be studied independently of their authors' intentions – but he was keen to see his new approach applied to philosophy at large.

Three books published in 1967, *Speech and Phenomena*, *Of Grammatology* and *Writing and Difference*, introduce and

PRETENTIOUS ... MOI?

Derrida's approach was not universally welcomed in academic circles. When Cambridge University wanted to award him an honorary degree in 1992, there were protests from a number of leading academics, who claimed that Derrida's contributions amounted to 'little more than semi-intelligible attacks upon the values of reason, truth, and scholarship'. Meanwhile, Chomsky (see p.171) accused him of using 'pretentious rhetoric' as a way of masking the simplicity of his ideas, and even Foucault (see p.169) was moved to say that Derrida wrote so obscurely that you couldn't follow what he was saying half the time, and that even if you did, but then criticized him, he would accuse you of being too stupid to understand.

Perhaps his critics were too stupid to understand. They were certainly outvoted and Derrida eventually received his honorary degree.

expand the basic concepts of deconstruction, which centre on theories of signification, indication, ideality and sense or meaning in general. To paraphrase the jargon, Derrida maintains that earlier philosophical systems have all been constructed on the basis of conceptual oppositions: for example, internal vs. external, transcendental vs. empirical, universal vs. particular.

One of these terms is always privileged over the other, which is then excluded. By analysing what's been excluded, Derrida shows that the preference for one term over the other is in fact groundless, because what's privileged has meaning only by virtue of being contrasted to what's excluded; it has no meaningful significance otherwise.

There is no grand system for Derrida, no generally applicable standards of truth in the outside world – critical textual analysis is all. And in highlighting the limitless possibilities of interpretation – which effectively means the impossibility of a definitive interpretation – Derrida draws attention to the fact that Western philosophy's attempts to establish certainty through reasoning have always been based on the shaky ground of promoting certain interpretations and suppressing others.

Some Metas, -isms
and -ologies

Atomism: Things can be understood once they have been broken down through analysis into distinct and independent components.

Conceptualism: Abstract concepts exist, but only in the mind.

Critical realism: There is some ultimate truth, but it is always limited in scope.

Deconstructionism: Analysis of philosophical and literary language through the study of the internal workings of concepts and language – i.e. the relations between meaning and the assumptions that lie behind forms of expression.

Deism: Belief in the existence of a supreme being or creator who does not intervene in the universe (cf. theism).

Deontology: Study of the nature of duty and obligation.

Determinism: All events and actions are ultimately determined by causes external to the will.

Dialectical materialism: Marxist view that political and historical events result from social conflict as a result of material needs, and can be seen as a series of contradictions and their resolutions.

Dualism: Division into two categories or elements (cf. monism).

Emotivism: Value judgements, especially ethical judgements, express emotions rather than representing facts.

Empiricism: All knowledge is based on experience derived from the senses.

Epistemology: Study of knowledge, particularly its methods, validity and scope – 'How do we know what we know?'

Existentialism: Existence of the individual as a free and responsible agent determining his or her own development through acts of the will.

Functionalism: Things are no more or less than the functions they fulfil in an overall system.

Humanism: Attaching prime importance to human rather than divine or supernatural matters.

Idealism: Objects of knowledge are dependent on the activity of the mind.

Ideology: System of ideas and ideals; negative connotations in Marxist theory, where dominant ideology is determined by ruling classes.

Libertarianism: Belief in free will rather than determinism (see above).

Logical positivism: Form of positivism (see below) that considers the only meaningful philosophical problems those that can be solved by logical analysis.

Materialism: Everything that exists is material or depends on matter for its existence.

Metaphilosophy: Theory about the nature of philosophy.

Metaphysics: Branch of philosophy concerned with first principles of things, including abstract concepts such as being and knowing.

Modernism: Modern ideas or styles that aim to break with traditional forms, particularly associated with the late nineteenth and early twentieth centuries.

Monism: There is only one substance or one world, and reality is one (cf. dualism).

Naturalism: Nature and the natural sciences lie at the root of all things, so there is no need for supernatural or spiritual explanations.

Nominalism: Universals or abstract concepts are just names, without any corresponding reality.

Ontology: Branch of metaphysics (see above) concerned with the nature of being.

Panentheism: God is greater than the universe, including and merging with it.

Pantheism: God is identified with the universe or the universe is a manifestation of God, making God and nature one.

Perspectivism: Ideas are rooted in particular perspectives, so there are any number of possible schemes for judging truth or value.

Phenomenalism: Human knowledge is confined to the appearances (phenomena) presented to the senses, or appearances are the foundation of knowledge.

Phenomenology: Science of phenomena as distinct from the nature of being; study of consciousness and objects of direct experience.

Positivism: System that recognizes only what can be scientifically verified or is capable of logical or mathematical proof.

Postmodernism: Late-twentieth-century style and concept in the arts, architecture and criticism; represents a departure from modernism and is characterized by the self-conscious use of earlier styles and conventions, a mixing of different artistic styles and media, and a general distrust of theories.

Rationalism: Reason rather than experience is the foundation of certainty in knowledge.

Realism: Universals or abstract concepts have an objective or absolute existence.

Relativism: Knowledge, truth and morality exist in relation to culture, society or historical context and so are not absolute.

Solipsism: The self is all that can be known to exist.

Structuralism: Human cognition, behaviour, culture etc. can be analysed by focusing on the contrasts between interrelated elements in a conceptual system.

Subjectivism: Knowledge is simply subjective, without external or objective truth.

Teleology: The explanation of phenomena by the purpose they serve rather than by postulated causes.

Theism: Belief in the existence of a god or gods, specifically a creator who intervenes in the universe (cf. deism).

Utilitarianism: Actions are right if they are useful or for the benefit of the majority.

Final Philosophy Paper

Answer the following questions in as many ways as you see fit — preferably with friends and a large glass of wine.

1. If I say this sentence is not true, am I telling the truth?

2. If a tree falls in the forest when no one is there, does it make a sound?

3. If all the swans I have ever seen are white, does that mean all swans are white?

4. If a lion could speak, would I understand what it was saying?

5. If my car is only a car because we've all agreed to call it a car and really it's just an intellectual construct, will it still cause a lot of damage if it crashes?

6. If the brakes fail on this car of mine as I'm driving towards a group of children crossing the road, am I justified in swinging the car up on to the pavement and knocking just one pedestrian down?

7. If the soles and heels of my shoes are replaced again and again are my shoes still the same shoes?

8. If I have a face transplant, am I still me?

9. Can a person travel back in time beyond when they were born?

10. Can a robot be human?

And finally a charming limerick by the theologian and crime writer Ronald Knox, inspired by Bishop Berkeley's *esse est percipi* concerns about being and perceiving:

> There was a young man who said, 'God
> Must find it exceedingly odd
> To think that the tree
> Should continue to be
> When there's no one about in the quad.'

Which prompted this anonymous reply:

> 'Dear Sir: Your astonishment's odd;
> I am *always* about in the quad.
> And that's why the tree
> Will continue to be
> Since observed by, Yours faithfully, God.'

Not a bad note on which to end ...

BIBLIOGRAPHY

◎◎

Berlin, Isaiah, *The Age of Enlightenment*, Mentor Books, New York, 1956

Blackburn, Simon (ed.), *Oxford Dictionary of Philosophy*, Oxford University Press, Oxford, 2008

Boardman, John, Griffin, Jasper, and Murray, Oswyn (eds), *The Oxford History of the Classical World*, Oxford University Press, Oxford, 1986

Chambers Biographical Dictionary, Chambers, Edinburgh, 1990

Chambers Dictionary of World History, Chambers, Edinburgh, 1994

Critchley, Simon, *Continental Philosophy: A Very Short Introduction*, Oxford University Press, Oxford and New York, 2001

Critchley, Simon, *The Book of Dead Philosophers*, Granta, London, 2009

Grayling, A. C., *The Meaning of Things*, Weidenfeld & Nicolson, London, 2001

Hampshire, Stuart, *The Age of Reason*, Mentor Books, New York, 1956

Honderich, Ted (ed.), *Oxford Companion to Philosophy*, Oxford University Press, Oxford, 2005

Kaufmann, Walter (ed.), *Existentialism from Dostoyevsky to Sartre*, New York, 1989 (extract from Jean-Paul Sartre lecture translated by Philip Mairet)

Knowles, Elizabeth (ed.), *Oxford Dictionary of Quotations*, Oxford University Press, Oxford, 2009

Kohl, Herbert, *The Age of Complexity*, Mentor Books, New York, 1965

Mautner, Thomas (ed.), *Penguin Dictionary of Philosophy*, Penguin Books, London, 1997

Monk, Ray, and Raphael, Frederic, *The Great Philosophers*, Weidenfeld & Nicolson, London, 2000

Oxford Dictionary of National Biography, Oxford University Press, Oxford, 2004

Pirie, Madsen, *101 Great Philosophers*, Continuum, London and New York, 2009

Rosenthal, M., and Yudin, P., *A Dictionary of Philosophy*, translated by Richard R. Dixon and Murad Saifulin, Progress Publishers, Moscow, 1967

Russell, Bertrand, *History of Western Philosophy*, George Allen & Unwin Ltd, London, 1961

Soanes, Catherine, and Stevenson, Angus (eds), *Oxford English Dictionary*, Oxford University Press, Oxford, 2005

Urmson, J. O., and Rée, Jonathan, *The Concise Encyclopedia of Western Philosophy & Philosophers*, Routledge, London and New York, 1989

INDEX

Principal locations for entries are shown in **bold**.